Free Yourself from Workplace Bullying

Become Bully-Proof and Regain Control of Your Life

Aryanne Oade

FREE Bonus Material on Workplace Bullying

- FREE access to a life-changing audio recording on recovery from workplace bullying

- FREE access to insightful, practical articles on responding effectively to bullying behaviour

- FREE access to manifestos on how to respond effectively to adversarial or bullying colleagues

- …and much more

Register for instant FREE access now at:

www.oadeassociates.com/downloads

Free Yourself from Workplace Bullying

Become Bully-Proof and Regain Control of Your Life

Aryanne Oade

www.oadeassociates.com

3

Oade Associates trading as Flourish
c/o Oxford Literary Consultancy
Suite 124
94 London Road
Oxford OX3 9FN

www.oadeassociates.com
mail@oadeassociates.com

ISBN 978-0-9931391-2-3
ePub ISBN 978-0-9931391-3-0

British Library Cataloguing in Publication Data
A catalogue record for this book is available from the British Library

Praise for *Free Yourself from Workplace Bullying*

This is a brilliant, insightful guide and toolbox for managing, escaping and recovering from bullying in the workplace. Because many of us have experienced bullying to some degree, wherever we have worked, this book is essential reading for everyone. It is a hugely valuable resource which sadly is needed now more than ever.

PROFESSOR DONAL MACINTYRE, Investigative Journalist and Broadcaster; Visiting Professor, School of Applied Criminology, Birmingham City University

This is a remarkable resource, full of useful advice on a very serious topic.

JOY ORPEN, Sunday Independent (Ireland)

Definitely a title to be aware of should you or anyone you know be unfortunate enough to have experienced bullying in the workplace.

SIMON TOSELAND, Safety and Health Practitioner Magazine

This is a seriously courageous — and much-needed — book. Aryanne shares her deep insights into the dynamics and impact of bullying. She offers a painfully accurate picture of the experience of being bullied, in a way that your head nods along in instinctive recognition of the truth of her words!

She gracefully empowers the bullied to take responsibility for resolving the situation without in any way 'blaming the victim'. Demonstrating her deep understanding of the emotional dynamics of bullying, and even drawing on modern neuro-science principles, she then guides those who are bullied in a practical and step-by-step way to reclaim their personal power and sense of dignity, and change their situation, no matter how hopeless it may seem.

A must-read for HR practitioners, managers and supervisors, coaches and professionals in the field of workplace bullying, and anyone who has experience of bullying.

BENNIE NAUDE, International Energy Psychology Expert www.deepliving.com

Easy-to-read and practical, this book gives effective, realistic help for those who are being bullied. The level of detail in the many well-crafted examples will help readers recognise their experience. The extensive toolkit provides a myriad of ideas for tackling bullying situations. This book reflects the author's many years helping employees tackle workplace bullying and is a useful, smart and thoughtfully written resource.

PROFESSOR CHARLOTTE RAYNER, Outgoing President: International Association of Workplace Bullying and Harassment; Visiting Professor of HR Management, Portsmouth Business School, Portsmouth University

This is exactly the book you need if you are feeling intimidated by a bully at work, are involved in HR or L&D, or are managing staff. It covers a comprehensive range of subjects to help develop understanding and strategies for dealing with workplace bullying. Each chapter has a useful summary of key facts which act as a quick reference point, and practical questions to challenge thinking and encourage self-reflection. This will not only help the reader develop their own knowledge, but empower those experiencing workplace bullying to take action.

TRACY WRAY, Deputy HR Director, Sheffield University

My experience as an HR Director in several large and complex organisations has left me in no doubt about the toxic effects of bullying on those who are targeted, and on the environment where bullying thrives. This very readable book is from an author with real insight into this difficult area. The book is full of practical tools to assist the reader to regain their power from the bully in a professional and dignified way, so that they can sustain their employment. I believe this is a must-read for anyone who is being bullied, or who needs to recover from workplace bullying. Importantly, it can also help those who are supporting these people and their organisations.

JACKIE GREEN FCIPD, Jackie Green Consulting Ltd; former HR Director for Leeds Teaching Hospitals NHS Trust and Royal Liverpool and Broadgreen University Hospitals; former Assistant CEO at The Housing Corporation

Most of us didn't expect to encounter bullying at work, thinking it'd be something we'd left behind with our school days. How wrong can we be! Unfortunately, bullying is not uncommon in the workplace. Aryanne's insightful book is an invaluable aid and toolkit to understanding, addressing and overcoming bullying behaviour. Through a selection of carefully crafted real life examples, she introduces the reader to an effective skill-set to protect against future bullying.

STEVE MOON, Independent Consultant and former Head of Energy, Global Project Finance, Bank of Ireland

Looking at real-life situations, Aryanne Oade deciphers the dynamics of workplace bullying and provides the reader with clear and simple solutions. She adroitly and sensitively highlights the nuanced character of bullying, sharing with readers an empowering set of tools through which to address it.

Her sound insights and keen, practice-based comprehension result in a book which is suitable for people across a wide variety of workplaces and job profiles. The book's focus is positive and progressive throughout, encouraging readers to learn new skills, internalise new ways of thinking about themselves and the bullying they are subject to, and answer thought-provoking self-awareness questions.

DR PREMILLA D'CRUZ, Professor of Organizational Behaviour at Indian Institute of Management Ahmedabad

I wish I'd had this book to hand early in my career. I'd have loved to have been able to apply Aryanne's qualitative tests for recognising bullying. This book will provide a treasure trove of useful information and help for anyone suffering from – or having suffered – bullying, or for those whose job involves managing bullying situations in their organisations.

JOHN ALLISON, former General Manager of a large publishing company

Free Yourself from Workplace Bullying was an award winning finalist for Best New Non-Fiction at the 2015 USA Best Book Awards, and at the Wishing Shelf Book Awards 2015. The book received an honourable mention in the same category at the 2015 London and New York Book Awards.

About the Author

Aryanne Oade works as a chartered psychologist, executive coach, workshop facilitator, author and interactive presenter. She has run her coaching and development business, Oade Associates, since 1994. Aryanne combines business psychology and professional acting in her projects. She lives on a non-commercial farm in Yorkshire, from where she runs her practice.
www.oadeassociates.com

Aryanne coaches clients to regain their self-confidence and self-esteem after workplace bullying, to learn how to use self-protective and self-preserving behaviour during an attack, and to alter the complex dynamics involved in bullying in their favour. She writes articles and speaks at conferences on recovery from workplace bullying. Aryanne is an Associate Fellow of the British Psychological Society.

Aryanne's six previous books include *Managing Workplace Bullying: How to Identify, Respond to and Manage Bullying Behaviour in the Workplace* (Palgrave Macmillan, 2009) and *Working in Adversarial Relationships: How to Operate Effectively in Relationships Characterised by Little Trust or Support* (Palgrave Macmillan 2010).

Acknowledgements and Dedication

I am grateful to a number of people for their input as I wrote this book.

I would like to acknowledge my clients, contacts and friends who allowed me to pick their brains at the start of the writing process. Due to my commitment to confidentiality, I am going to mention each of you by your first name only. My thanks go to June, Paul, Louise, Anna, Sarah, Joe, Lizzie, Phil and Barbara for their generosity of spirit, for making time for me in their busy schedules, and for their willingness to share their experiences of workplace bullying with me. I'd also like to thank Barbara, Sally and Steve for reading sections of the typescript for me early on, and for their encouragement and enthusiasm for the book.

My heartfelt thanks go to June, who acted throughout the writing process as my unofficial editor. Her attention to detail, knowledge of grammar, suggestions for additional ideas and angles to include in the book, and her experience as someone who has been bullied were invaluable to me. Her input made the book a better book.

Free Yourself from Workplace Bullying is dedicated to Sal.

Note from the Author

This book focuses on how to recognise and tackle grooming and bullying behaviour in the workplace so that you can regain control at the time of an attack. In the book I offer you, the reader, insights, tools and strategies which I have honed over many years of working with my clients to resolve the issues created by incidents of workplace bullying.

I hope you find the book a valuable resource from which to select tactics to help you effectively alter the bullying dynamic which plays out between you and the person bullying you. However, in addition to applying the lessons from this book, you may also want to contact your employer's HR department or consult your organisation's anti-bullying policy, should these options be open to you. I recommend that, if you are significantly impacted by experiences of workplace bullying, you work with a professional coach or therapist experienced in enabling recovery from bullying.

Also by Aryanne Oade:

*Managing Workplace Bullying: How to Identify, Respond to and
Manage Bullying Behaviour in the Workplace*
(Palgrave Macmillan 2009)

*Working in Adversarial Relationships: Operating Effectively in
Relationships Characterised by Little Trust or Support*
(Palgrave Macmillan 2010)

*Managing Politics at Work: The Essential Toolkit for Identifying and
Managing Political Behaviour in the Workplace*
(Palgrave Macmillan 2009)

*Managing Challenging Clients: Building Effective Relationships
with Difficult Customers*
(Palgrave Macmillan 2011)

*Building Influence in the Workplace: How to Gain and Retain
Influence at Work*
(Palgrave Macmillan 2010)

*Starting and Running a Coaching Business: The Complete Guide to
Setting Up and Managing a Coaching Practice*
(How To Books 2008)

Detailed Chapter Contents

- Case study 1: personal power
- Analysing the dynamics in case study 1: personal power
- Exploring the bullying dynamic
- Summary of key points from the chapter
- Questions for you to consider
- Next chapter

- The devastating effects of workplace bullying
- Toxic shame: blaming yourself
- Avoiding: a common response to workplace bullying
- Complying: a second common response to workplace bullying
- The consequences of avoiding and complying
- Confronting your powerlessness and toxic thinking
- Exercise 1: tackling self-defeating thinking and toxic beliefs
- Case study 2: paralysed
- Analysing the dynamics in case study 2: paralysed
- Feeling abandoned, waiting for rescue
- Summary of key points from the chapter
- Questions for you to consider
- Next chapter

- What is grooming?
- Early warning signs
- Mishandling the moment
- What bullies look for when they groom
- Case study 3: groomed
- Analysing the dynamics in case study 3: groomed
- Handling grooming effectively
- Putting the issue back to the bully
- Summary of key points from the chapter
- Questions for you to consider
- Next chapter

- Unresolved authority issues
- Inside the mind of a bullying team member
- Active aggression
- Passive aggression
- The strategy of active aggression
- The strategy of passive aggression
- What bullying team members want, and what they need
- Asserting your authority
- Case study 5: lies and innuendo
- Analysing the dynamics in case study 5: lies and innuendo
  - Need for approval
  - Calculated attack
  - Double standards
  - Resisting falsehood and slander
  - Resolving authority issues
- Summary of key points from the chapter
- Questions for you to consider
- Next chapter

- Observing bullying in your team meeting
- Case study 6: negative impact
- Analysing the dynamics in case study 6: negative impact
  - Mishandling a campaign of bullying
  - Refusing to become a passive enabler
  - Active involvement
  - Uncompromising tone
  - Appearing resolute, standing together
  - Offering life-giving support
- Summary of key points from the chapter
- Questions for you to consider
- Next chapter

- A situation of on-going abuse
- The issues involved in leaving your job

- The issues involved in remaining in your job
- The role of feelings, needs, resources and choices in making a positive decision
- Unresolved situations
- Your feelings, needs, resources and choices
- Developing a positive mind-set
- Your positive mind-set: questions for you to consider
- Final thoughts

Introduction

What You Will Get From this Book

Workplace Bullying is a Fact of Life

Workplace bullying happens every day in workplaces up and down the country. Anyone can be targeted: people who appear to be quite assertive, people who lack confidence, people who have significant organisational authority, people who don't. Not everyone who is targeted will become subject to a campaign of workplace bullying. But many will and, sadly, workplace bullying is a fact of life.

You have probably picked up this book because these issues have become real for you. Maybe you are unfortunate enough to be subject to bullying behaviour in your workplace right now. Or maybe you think you are being targeted but aren't sure. You may be concerned that you could be bullied at some point in the future. Or maybe you want to access effective assistance on behalf of a friend, family member or colleague who is subject to bullying behaviour in their workplace. While the book is written to 'you' the reader, it will also be of value to those of you who do not have first-hand experience of workplace bullying but are involved in managing incidents in your role as human resources or dignity at work advisors, as strategists and policy formulators, and as coaches who work with clients on issues surrounding workplace bullying.

What each of you needs is a resource which will show you what workplace bullying is, how it affects each of you, and how to handle it in an effective, self-protective and self-preserving way. This is exactly what this book will do.

What This Book Will Do for You

Working with the text and exercises in this book will enable you to learn how to:

- Protect yourself against bullying behaviour *at the time of an attack.*

- Understand the ways in which being targeted may have affected what you think, feel and believe, as well as how you behave at work.

- Prevent a workplace bully from successfully grooming or targeting you in the future.

- Re-gain your confidence after an experience of workplace bullying.

- Support someone you know who is vulnerable to being targeted, and doesn't know what to do to protect themselves.

This book represents a distillation of powerful, proven techniques. It will provide you with information and insight into why you, or your contact, may be vulnerable to being bullied. It will provide you with practical strategies through which to protect yourself from future attack. It will enable you to develop wisdom about the nature of the dynamic that a bully is trying to create in their interactions with you. It will challenge you to learn new skills, develop new strategies and decide where to place the boundaries around your inner self and your work so that you protect yourself effectively from bullying behaviour.

My wish is that, as you read and work with the exercises in this book, you learn to how to send a message back to anyone who targets you that you will be a difficult person with whom to create a bullying dynamic.

> **This book will show you how to handle incidents of workplace bullying simply and effectively.**

The Journey Ahead of You

As you work with this book you will be embarking on a journey of self-discovery. Only you can do the actual work of travelling that path but this book can guide you along the way. Your journey will result in you learning about the values, assumptions and beliefs which drive your behaviour when you are subject to bullying, and when you are not. Your journey may involve both your workplace self and your personal self. It is the experiences of your workplace self which have lead you to pick up this book. But as you read it and work with the exercises in it, you may find that your personal self becomes involved in the journey too.

The work you are embarking on may take time and it will take commitment. You cannot create a ten-year-old whiskey in two years, and you cannot develop the wisdom, inter-personal craft and intra-personal resilience you need to handle bullying behaviour effectively in two days. But you can develop all these attributes, and you can do so in much less time than you think.

> **Your journey may involve both your workplace and your personal selves.**

My Experience Coaching Clients to Detoxify from Workplace Bullying

For more than twenty years, I have coached and worked with many clients whose self-esteem and self-confidence plummeted following experiences of workplace bullying. As part of the coaching process, I ask each client to step back from their experience of being bullied and tell me about the meetings with the bully which were most destructive. I then re-create the very dynamics that were so challenging for my client to handle in a series of enacted scenarios. During these scenarios, I ask my clients to put themselves back into an abusive situation in the safety of the coaching room, learn to handle the dynamics self-protectively, and practise the behaviour they need to learn to put the issues back to the bully at the time of an attack.

I coach them to understand the links between the inner world of their thoughts, fears and beliefs and their inter-personal behaviour during an encounter with the bully. They learn to regain control, preserve their personal power and handle previously challenging situations simply and effectively. The techniques in this book come out of my work in helping many clients to handle, simply and straightforwardly, situations which they had previously found abusive. My objective in writing this book is not to tell you what to do in any of the situations you may experience. Rather, it is to show you what I know has worked for my clients as they have climbed out of the mire of powerlessness and despair that is so often a consequence of workplace bullying.

Recovery from Trauma

Some of my clients were so traumatised by their experiences that they were unable to work for a time and others became anxious at the very thought of setting foot in their workplaces. All of them recovered. Each of them amazed and delighted themselves as they discovered depths of personal resources which they did not know they had. And, for each of these courageous clients, it was when they involved their personal self in their recovery path that they developed levels of self-esteem and self-confidence which were much higher than before their experience of workplace bullying. They all got their energy and enthusiasm back – and were more resilient and better resourced than before they were bullied.

Commitment to the journey was vital for each of these clients. And it may be for you too. Don't hesitate or become discouraged. If you waver, or if you start the journey and fall away, you may undermine yourself. Even if the process means that, for a time at least, your journey takes up more of your thoughts, time and energy than you would like, keep going. The outcome of your journey will be worth it as you:

- Learn the skills, tools and inter-personal strategies you need to handle bullying behaviour effectively.

- Develop a bully-proof mind-set which will prevent you from being successfully targeted in the future.

- Improve your levels of resilience and your capacity to handle previously stressful bullying dynamics with ease.

- Confront bullying behaviour quickly and effectively, clarify the boundaries and put the relevant issues back to the bully.

All of these inter-personal issues, and many more, are addressed in this book.

The Bullying Dynamic

Many of you who are, or have been, subject to workplace bullying will recognise a pattern of:

- The bully using aggressive, intimidating behaviour towards you.

- You feeling afraid and being unable to say what you want to say, or do what you want to do.

- The bully learning that their use of aggression successfully controls you to some extent, which encourages them to use these tactics again.

- A cycle of behaviour developing between the two of you whereby the bully intimidates you, you outwardly comply with their wishes, but inwardly fume.

Many of my clients were distressed and overwhelmed when they first started to work with me. Often this was due to the disconnect between how they FELT at the time of an attack – furious, hurt, afraid – and what they DID – tried to get the encounter over with as soon as possible. They blamed themselves. They castigated themselves for not having handled the worst bullying situations more effectively. And their berating of themselves added to the overwhelm they experienced from having been subject to unwarranted aggression at work.

Should these descriptions resonate with you, you have my utmost compassion and my assurance that you can recover when you fully commit to the journey.

The Bullying Dynamic and Your Self-Image

Much of the toxic impact of bullying arises from the negative judgements you can make about yourself because you are being bullied. The good news is that it is possible to take complete control over how you think about yourself. You can develop how you see yourself with:

- Time to reflect on what has happened to you and what your experiences mean to you.

- Relevant input to challenge the unhelpful, negative beliefs and thoughts you have generated about yourself as a result of being subject to bullying behaviour.

- Suggestions for effective mental skills and strategies which will enable you to create a more positive self-image to replace the toxic shame you have generated because you were bullied.

All of these intra-personal issues, and many more, are addressed in this book.

> **You need to reject the negative beliefs you have developed about yourself as a result of being bullied.**

What Else This Book Will Do For You

This book will help you get your experiences into perspective and make a clear distinction between what is your responsibility – to self-care and self-protect when confronted with bullying behaviour – and what is not: the bully's aggression. It will encourage you to accept that the bully's aggression is not being provoked by you, but rather is being generated because of *pre-existing issues in the life of the bully.*

You did not deserve to be subject to bullying behaviour. You did not encourage it. Nor did you do or say anything which caused the aggression you experienced, or fear you may experience in the future. Responsibility for all of these issues sits with the person using bullying behaviour – not with you.

This book will encourage you to:

- Identify bullying behaviour at work early on, so you can mentally prepare for an attack should you be targeted.

- Select effective inter-personal strategies for retaining control when you are attacked.

- Understand why these strategies and tactics are effective.

- Understand the dynamic at the heart of a workplace bullying relationship, so you can prevent it from being created or interrupt it should it already be in place.

- Recognise the self-defeating patterns of thinking and behaviour which you may have adopted as a result of being subject to bullying behaviour.

- Understand why colleagues who witness bullying behaviour often don't speak up in support of the person being targeted.

- Recognise why influential people in organisations so often fail to tackle bullying behaviour and thereby enable it.

You are NOT responsible for having been bullied. What happened to you is NOT your fault. You are NOT to blame. You were NOT bullied because you are you.

Longer Case Studies and Shorter Examples

Throughout the book you will find longer case studies which illustrate the themes of the preceding section of text, and shorter examples which capture specific key points. Each case study or shorter example is a realistic depiction of an incident of workplace bullying. Some of the dynamics portrayed in these scenarios are based on incidents which my clients have related to me, and in each case my client has given me permission to include a fictionalised, anonymised version of their experience in the book. Other scenarios are a blend of a number of incidents which I have fictionalised and anonymised. I am absolutely committed to permanent confidentiality for each of my clients, and have written each of the real-life instances in a way which fully protects the identity of my clients.

Each case study or shorter example highlights:

- The behaviours and tactics used by the workplace bully in each scenario.

- How these behaviours impact the bully's target.

- Well-intentioned, but ineffective responses which the target uses to try to retain some control in their encounter with the bully.

- Issues in the person's life which render them vulnerable to being targeted.

- Effective responses which the target could employ to preserve some or all of their personal power at the time of an attack.

Periodic Text Boxes

As you will have noticed, throughout the book you will find key points highlighted in bold in page-width text boxes. I have highlighted these key points because they are crucially important messages I would like you to absorb. The page-width text boxes include messages about:

- Attitudes to adopt to help you develop a bully-proof mind set.

- Self-defeating thoughts and beliefs which you may have fallen into as a result of being bullied.

- More healthy, realistic, accurate and life-giving thoughts and beliefs with which to replace them, and which better serve your interests.

- What to say and do at the time of an attack to retain control, put the issues back to the bully, and preserve your personal power.

At the end of each chapter, you will find a set of questions which encourage you to apply the material from that chapter to your own experience. These questions give you an opportunity to re-visit incidents of workplace bullying and devise a more effective way of handling similar encounters in the future.

Your Journey to Health and Wellbeing

I hope you find this resource invaluable as you come to terms with experiences of workplace bullying, recover fully from them, and prepare yourself to become bully-proof against future attacks.

With my best wishes for the journey ahead.

Aryanne Oade
Ch. Psychol. AFBPsS
www.oadeassociates.com

Chapter 1
What Constitutes Workplace Bullying?

The Difference between True Bullying and Aggressive, Non-Bullying Behaviour

An Experience of Aggression at Work

You may know for sure that you have been subject to bullying behaviour. You simply know that you were targeted, and subject to coercive or aggressive behaviour in your workplace. You have been impacted in ways that are more or less debilitating, and you are concerned that you are vulnerable to being targeted again. Others of you are in a situation of on-going abuse. You recognise that you are under attack from a workplace bully, and that the bullying is negatively impacting you right now. All of you want to come to terms with what has happened to you and learn to protect yourself simply and effectively. You want to know what to do should there be another incident.

However, some of you may simply be unsure whether you were bullied or not. You may have had colleagues and co-workers present while you were subject to aggression. These colleagues and co-workers witnessed what occurred but have carried on as normal, as if nothing untoward has happened in their workplace. Their apparent lack of concern for you, and their apparent lack of anxiety or chagrin towards the person who bullied you, has put doubt into your mind about whether what you experienced was unreasonable or not. You can't be sure whether the aggression that you experienced constitutes workplace bullying or not. You may have read other books on the subject. You may have confided your experiences to friends or to workplace contacts who know the person who behaves aggressively towards you. Your contacts may have told you to 'get over it', 'toughen up' or 'let it slide,' demonstrating a lack of understanding about what happened to you and what it means to you. You are confused and want some information so you can make an assessment about what you did experience, what it means to you and how to handle similar incidents should they occur in the future.

In this chapter we will explore:

- The behaviours and intentions that constitute workplace bullying.

- The difference between workplace bullying and aggressive but non-bullying behaviour.

- The dynamics involved in an incident of workplace bullying.

- The central issue of how to preserve your personal power at the time of an attack.

We will examine each of these issues in a series of practical examples and case studies. Let's start with a definition of what workplace bullying is, so you can step back from your situation and look at it with fresh eyes.

A Definition of Workplace Bullying

In my view workplace bullying involves:

- One-off, frequent or repeated personal attacks which you find emotionally hurtful or professionally harmful.

- A deliberate attempt by the bully to undermine your ability to carry out your work, or to injure your reputation, or to undermine your self-esteem and self-confidence.

- A deliberate attempt by the bully to remove personal power from you and keep this power for themselves.

I consider that all three elements in the above definition need to be present at the same time for any incident of aggression at work to be classed as workplace bullying. I think this is true whether the aggression is subtle and indirect - such as a bully deciding to quietly slander you behind your back in an attempt to undermine your reputation - or outright and obvious - such as an angry verbal attack orchestrated against you by a bully during a one-to-one encounter or a group meeting.

You'll note that the third bullet introduces the term personal power. Personal power refers to your right to choose for yourself how you will behave. It is your right to decide for yourself what you think, what you say, what you do and what values you act in accordance with. It is personal to you, and individual to you. Every one of us has the same potential for exercising personal power. But not all of us know how to use that potential wisely at the time of an attack. If you are vulnerable to attack, it is vital that you learn how to send back the message to a would-be bully that you know how to protect yourself and preserve your personal power.

We will consider personal power and how to retain it in detail throughout subsequent chapters. These chapters will identify a range of proven behavioural strategies you can use at the time of an attack, all of which will prove effective at enabling you to handle aggressive emotion as well. Now let's continue to clarify what does and what does not constitute bullying at work.

Workplace bullying involves a deliberate attempt to hurt you emotionally, injure your reputation, or undermine your self-esteem and self-confidence.

What Constitutes Bullying Behaviour?

I make a distinction between:

- A person who occasionally or regularly gets it wrong and uses an aggressive tone, overbearing body language, or furious words, written or spoken, to convey anger at work.

And:

- A person who is responsible for an incident of true workplace bullying.

The former may involve behaviour which is totally out of line, very upsetting and completely unacceptable. But, unless it involves a deliberate attempt to injure another person, combined with a deliberate attempt to remove power from that person and retain that control for themselves, then no matter how regrettable or damaging to a workplace relationship the incident may be, I wouldn't consider it to be an incident of workplace bullying.

Workplace bullying is about power. It involves a person seeking to remove power from you and keep it for themselves. The form of power they wish to remove from you may vary. It could include your organisational influence or it may be the personal power that comes from feeling confident and able in your job. They may do this by attacking you personally, they may do it by attacking your performance, or they may do it by undermining your credibility and reputation among your colleagues and co-workers. Some bullies may use a combination of all of these tactics, but in each case a true workplace bully wants to remove your power from you and retain this control for themselves.

Consider the following short examples:

- A porter in a busy hotel begins to make cutting and crude remarks to female members of the reception staff team every time he collects or deposits suitcases from the luggage room behind the reception desk. He makes his remarks as he walks directly behind a receptionist en route to the luggage room, using a soft and deliberate tone. Then he moves smartly into the luggage room. A few seconds later he re-emerges from the luggage room, walks out from behind the reception desk and speaks in a warm and hearty voice to the customers waiting for him in the lobby. Each incident is over swiftly. Each is unexpected from the point of view of the female member of the reception staff who is invariably fully occupied serving a customer at the time, and is aware that there is a queue of tired-looking customers waiting to be served.

- A marketing manager in a call centre decides to arrange a meeting with the IT staff member who maintains the telephone communications systems her team members use. The IT staff member does not report to her, but his desk is on her floor next to her staff, so he can respond quickly to their requests for IT support. The marketing manager calls the IT staff member into her office, warmly invites him to sit down and, when he is off guard and seated, tells him she is monitoring his performance and has kept a log of the emails he has sent to her staff members.

Let's apply the definition to each of these two examples to determine whether they are incidents of workplace bullying. In the first example, the hotel porter directs cutting and crude comments at whichever female reception staff member happens to be on duty that day. Is this an example of workplace bullying? Yes, it is. It fulfils all three aspects of the definition. Let's examine them one by one:

- Firstly, the attacks are *personally directed* at individual female reception staff members. Each attack is a whispered insult dropped into the ear of the female receptionist in question, delivered behind her back, as she carries out her duties. These are personal attacks, cunningly handled.

- Secondly, they take the form of wounding comments designed to *injure the self-esteem and confidence* of the target. Each attack consists of personally offensive and crude comments which are hurtful and insulting. Each attack is also planned to isolate the target. By stealthily dropping comments into her ear from behind, it is possible that no one other than the target is aware an attack has been carried out.

- Thirdly, the porter makes each incident about his power *over* his colleague. He sets up every incident to make it very difficult for the target to defend themselves: they are always busy serving customers, the porter stands behind them as he verbally attacks them, he moves away quickly into the luggage room to reduce the target's opportunity to retort, and on exiting the luggage room he immediately alters his demeanour to appear hearty and apparently customer-focused as he re-engages with the customers whose luggage he is handling. This is an example of true workplace bullying. It consists of a series of personal insults which are designed to intimidate and undermine those subject to them, and which are about the porter's desire to exert power over a specific group of colleagues: the female receptionists in the hotel.

In the second example, the call centre marketing manager decides to arrange a meeting with the IT staff member who works on her team's communications equipment. She calls him into her office, puts him at ease and then stuns him by telling him that she is monitoring his performance and has been collecting his emails. Is this an example of workplace bullying or is this a conscientious marketing manager safeguarding the quality of IT work being done in her department? Let's apply the three-part definition to find out.

- Does the marketing manager orchestrate a personal attack on the IT team member, one that he would find *personally or professionally damaging*? Yes, she does. She attacks his work out of the blue without there being any context which he knows about that would justify his performance being called into question.

- Does she deliberately try and *undermine his ability to carry out his work, injure his reputation, or undermine his self-esteem and self-confidence*? Yes, she does all three of these things. By setting up a bogus 'inquiry' into the standard of the work he has been doing, she attacks him professionally and personally. The IT staff member is a hardworking and diligent man. The call centre marketing manager knows full well that the quality of his work is something he takes pride in and that, in his mind, to attack the quality of his work *is* to attack him personally. Her attack on his work is quite calculated.

- Does she do this to *remove personal power from him and keep this control for herself?* Absolutely. She makes her attack about her power *over* him. His work has not been the subject of debate up until that moment. He has not made any errors or mistakes that have been drawn to his attention by her or anybody else. The attack happens in her office. She sets it up by being warm and welcoming so she can lull him into a false sense of security, and then she attacks him out of the blue. She gives him two pieces of information: that she is monitoring his performance and that she is keeping a log of the emails he sends to her staff. Let's look carefully at the implications behind these two pieces of information. The first implies that she has the organisational authority to 'monitor' his performance which suggests that his departmental manager is involved in the monitoring exercise.

The second suggests that there is such concern about his conduct and work quality that a decision has been made to collect his emails and scrutinise them. The overall tenor of the two pieces of information is enough to put tremendous fear and anxiety into the mind of the IT team member, and to cause him to consider that his work must be of such low quality that monitoring is justified. He may be so upset that it may not occur to him that he hasn't done anything wrong, that the monitoring exercise is fictional, that the call centre marketing manager has not collected his emails and doesn't have automatic access to her team's inboxes, and that his own manager thinks he is doing a great job. His anxiety levels may well be so high that he is simply floored, and the call centre marketing manager can then proceed to bully him whenever she wants to.

In both of these examples one colleague bullies another. In both of these examples, all three aspects of the definition are present in the way the bully plans, sets up and executes their attacks. Both are examples of true workplace bullying, although the dynamics are very different across the two cases.

So, to recap: for an incident of aggression at work to be true workplace bullying there needs to be:

- A personal element to the attack on you, in that you experience it as being personally directed at you.

- A deliberate attempt by the bully to undermine or injure you as a person; or to undermine or injure you professionally; or both.

- A desire on the part of the bully to make the encounter about their power *over* you.

This latter point is crucial. Some bullies have greater organisational status than the colleagues they target. They are your supervisors, line managers and senior executives. Other bullies do not have greater organisational status than you. In fact, some of you are managers who have been targeted by your team members; some of you have been targeted by members of your peer group; and some of you have experience of your patients or their family or friends targeting you as you care for them in your role as a medical practitioner or healthcare worker. In these latter cases, the bully attempts to remove personal power and influence from you even though their organisational status may be equal to or less than yours or, in the case of patients, they are actually in the process of receiving a much-needed service from you. In each case, the bully wants to remove power from you and retain that control for themselves.

But what about circumstances where one co-worker uses aggression at work – even raging aggression – but the incident is not about their desire to remove power from you and retain it for themselves?

Workplace bullying is about the bully seeking to remove power from you and keep it for themselves.

Key Differences between True Workplace Bullying and Non-Bullying Aggressive Behaviour at Work

Consider the following short examples:

- A garden centre worker is fed up with having to neatly re-stack the centre's collection of heavy pot tubs and containers at the end of each day. He thinks it's a pointless task as the following day a new set of customers will come along and move the tubs leaving them in another mess. At the end of a particularly tiring day in which he only had twenty minutes lunch break he notices that the tubs and containers are strewn about the pathway to the indoor shrubs, and represent a health and safety hazard. He wants to go home and is torn between rearranging the tubs and simply leaving them. He notices a colleague walking towards him. He snaps. He points towards the tubs and shouts angrily at his colleague to 'stop slacking and sort out that mess'.

- A credit controller in a busy investment bank is reviewing a print-out of the day's transactions, as she does each evening. In the past she has twice found a specific error attributable to her deputy, and has twice made a point of taking him through it the following day to show him how the item ought to be accounted for. Each time, he apologised and appeared to take the feedback on board, only to make the exact same error again. On noticing the same error a third time, she leaps up from her desk, strides across the open plan area outside her office and makes a beeline for the deputy controller's console. Once there she rages at him, telling him in an arrogant and high-handed manner in full hearing of the entire department that he is a moron who can't get anything right.

Let's apply the above definition to each of these two examples to determine whether they are incidents of true workplace bullying or of non-bullying but, nonetheless, unacceptable aggression.

In the first example, a garden centre worker loses his temper at the end of a busy day, and rounds on a colleague. He shouts angrily at his colleague to 'stop slacking and sort out that mess' when the colleague in question hadn't created the mess and wasn't responsible for sorting it out. Is this an incident of true workplace bullying or an example of one colleague being unreasonably aggressive towards another but with no intention to bully? Let's apply the three-part definition to find out.

- Does the tired garden centre worker orchestrate a *personal attack* on his colleague, one that he would find personally or professionally damaging? Yes, he does. He calls his colleague a slacker, something which is personally unfair and uncalled for.

- Does he deliberately try and *undermine his colleague's ability to carry out his work, injure his reputation, or undermine his self-esteem and self-confidence?* Not really. He takes out his own frustration and fatigue on someone who simply happens to be there, but he doesn't do it to injure him. He does it to vent. It's an unkind thing to do, and may well hurt the colleague he shouts at, but it is not an intentional attempt to wound him.

- Thirdly, does the garden centre worker attempt to *remove personal power from his colleague and keep this control for himself?* No. This incident is not about power. It is about one person's inability to handle their own fatigue and frustration and their consequent poor behaviour towards their colleague. A clear apology is called for, along with a clear decision never to behave like that again, but not a complaint about workplace bullying.

In the second example, a credit controller snaps after finding the same error for a third time. She marches across the open plan office towards the desk of the person she holds culpable for the error and verbally assaults him in front of the entire department. She calls him a moron who can't get anything right and uses an arrogant and demeaning tone to do so. Is this an incident of true workplace bullying or an example of an under-skilled manager messing up? Let's apply the three-part definition to find out.

- Does the credit controller orchestrate a *personal attack* on her colleague, one that he would find personally or professionally damaging? Absolutely, yes. She is rude, aggressive and demeaning towards her colleague, and does it all in front of the entire department. The deputy could easily feel humiliated and belittled by the incident. The rest of the members of the team learn that the credit controller is a ruthless adversary when roused, and they will all have to consider whether they want to work for such a woman.

- Does the credit controller deliberately try and *undermine her colleague's ability to carry out his work, injure his reputation, or undermine his self-esteem and self-confidence*? Her attack on him would certainly have upset him deeply. It may have dented his self-esteem and may have resulted in him being unable to concentrate for the rest of that day and perhaps a portion of the next day too. But was it deliberate? Was it an intentionally planned attack, the sole purpose of which was to undermine him? I don't think so. The credit controller snaps because her high standards of meticulous and error-free work are challenged by the same error being made three times in a row by the same team member. She allows her anger to dominate the actions she takes in the next thirty seconds, and demonstrates a woeful lack of self-control as she rounds on her team member in public in a humiliating show of aggression. She may well have damaged her relationship with him, perhaps to the point of ending it, but she does not take these actions as part of a planned and intentional campaign of bullying him. She takes these actions because she lacks the intra-personal skills to handle her own aggression, because she lacks the sense to realise that the errors being made by her deputy do not give her justification for attacking him in public, and because she hasn't managed to motivate her team member to produce error-free work. Sure, she can be thoroughly fed up that he hasn't accepted the need to work to higher standards, and she can have a frank and clear discussion with him about his failure to do so, should she wish. But that discussion needs to be behind closed doors, and needs to be conducted in a tone consistent with giving constructive feedback in a business environment. It must not be handled in an unskilled, abusive or aggressive tone. The credit controller clearly gets a lot wrong in her handling of this incident. But, while she may have humiliated him and irreparably damaged her relationship with him, she has not deliberately set out to bully her deputy.

- Thirdly, does the credit controller attempt to *remove personal power from her colleague and keep this control for herself?* No, her attack on him is not designed to remove power from him. She has not thought that far ahead. But, her deputy may well feel disabled and humiliated as his boss berates him in public. As a consequence of her dangerous mishandling of the moment, the credit controller may well lose her deputy's goodwill and commitment, and the goodwill and commitment of everyone in the team who witnesses the incident, or subsequently hears about it from someone who observed it. The consequences for the credit controller of displaying so much raw aggression may well be considerable and may take a number of months to play out as team members decide to work for someone else, or put their effort and energy into other parts of their lives, doing just enough to get by during the day. She may find it very hard to recover from this serious error of judgement and will need to learn quickly if she is to continue to manage people. But this particular manager is not responsible for an incident of workplace bullying.

Personal Thresholds

At the end of this first chapter, and alongside the definition of workplace bullying we have been considering, let's briefly examine the issue of personal thresholds. Each of you has a threshold that is personal to you which, if it is breached by aggression, renders you vulnerable to feeling disoriented, alarmed, afraid, anxious, hurt or confused. Your personal threshold could be breached by one incident of aggression which you experienced as particularly punishing, or it may be breached by a number of incidents each of which was insufficient by itself to cause you distress but which cumulatively did exactly that.

However, behaviour which you experience as unacceptable and hurtful may be shrugged off by another colleague as irritating but not damaging. In other words, the same behaviour which you experienced as debilitating apparently does not harm a colleague. Some of my clients have used this fact to beat themselves up and, in case you are tempted to do the same, I would like to pre-empt you by re-framing the issue. It simply means that your personal threshold is in a different place to the colleague who appears more resilient than you. It does NOT mean that you are being over-sensitive. It is the behaviour of the bully that requires scrutiny – not your reaction to it.

One of the aims of this book is to enable you to use behaviour which retains you control in the moment of an attack, so that you remain buoyant when subject to aggression. By applying the messages in this book, you will develop the bandwidth within which you comfortably withstand aggression without experiencing it as disabling. Your personal threshold will be breached less often, and with less distress, and you will become more resilient.

Summary of the Key Points from the Chapter

Not every incident involving aggression at work constitutes workplace bullying. Workplace bullying is about power. It's about one colleague or co-worker's desire to make their relationship with you about their power *over* you, something they do for the length of the time they target you.

That is not the same as the person who gets it wrong at work and is aggressive towards colleagues or co-workers because they mis-manage their own emotions that day. That person allows their anger to dominate their behaviour towards you, and uses the

---

interaction to vent their feelings. This approach may be very upsetting and require a genuine apology. In some egregious cases it may do so much damage that the working relationship is no longer viable. But these incidents are different from true workplace bullying because they are not about power. In true workplace bullying, the bully wants to remove your power from you and retain that control for themselves.

During an incident of true workplace bullying, there are three distinct factors at play simultaneously:

- The attack is experienced personally by you, and is emotionally hurtful or professionally harmful.
- The bully deliberately attempts to undermine your ability to carry out your work, or to injure your reputation, or to undermine your self-esteem and self-confidence.
- The bully wants to remove personal power from you and keep this power for themselves.

Learning how to send back the message to a bully that you know how to protect yourself and preserve your personal power at the time of an attack is a key learnable skill. The skills described in the book will prove valuable if you need to handle aggressive behaviour at work as well as bullying behaviour.

My goal in writing this book is that those of you vulnerable to attack will learn how to protect yourselves and preserve your personal power as you consider the practical examples and work through the exercises and questions. Resilience is a learned skill, and as you develop your skills in remaining resilient under pressure, so your personal threshold will not be subject to breach by aggressive behaviour – and you will not feel disabled or disoriented – as often as at present.

Questions for You to Consider

In this chapter we have been examining the difference between aggressive, non-bullying behaviour and true workplace bullying. You may now want to apply the distinctions made in this chapter to your own situation by responding to the following questions. You can jot down your answer to each in the space below it.

Call to mind a recent incident in which you were subject to aggression in your workplace.

1. What happened during the incident you have called to mind?

2. What impact did the incident have on you? What impact did it have on your ability to carry out your work that day and subsequently?

3. What impact did the incident have on your working relationship with the colleague or co-worker who was aggressive towards you?

4. To what extent do you think that incident represents a personal attack on you?

5. To what extent do you think that the incident was designed to injure you personally or professionally, or designed to undermine your ability to carry out your work competently?

6. To what extent do you think that the incident was about a desire on the part of your colleague or coworker to remove power from you and retain that control for themselves?

7. Looking back at what you have written, to what extent do you now regard what happened as an incident of true workplace bullying or as an incident of aggressive, non-bullying behaviour?

Next Chapter

Chapter 2 will continue to explore the actions and behaviours that constitute workplace bullying, this time focusing on what bullies want to achieve, the nature of the bullying dynamic and how to retain personal power at the time of an attack.

Chapter 2
Getting to Grips with
Workplace Bullying

The Dynamics at Play in a Bullying
Relationship at Work

An Experience of Workplace Bullying

You recognise that you have been subject to bullying behaviour at work. You feel disabled, confused and hurt. You have to work alongside the bully and cannot do your job effectively without some interactions with them. They may be your line manager or someone else senior in the organisation. They may be a peer or someone in your team. They could even be a client, customer or patient: someone who looks to you for a service. Whatever the nature of the relationship you recognise that your colleague, co-worker or client uses bullying behaviour occasionally, intermittently or every time they encounter you.

In this chapter we will get to grips with the nature of a bullying relationship at work. We will consider why some colleagues and co-workers decide to bully, and examine the role that envy and jealousy can play in incidents of workplace bullying. We will describe some of the tactics employed by bullies during their campaigns, and explore the nature of the bullying dynamic which is at the heart of a bullying relationship. The chapter will complete by exploring the central theme of personal power: what is it and how to retain it at the time of an attack. Each of the principles and key points in the chapter will be illustrated in a practical example or longer case study.

Let's begin by considering why a colleague or co-worker might decide to change their relationship with you from one which is about two people working together into one which is about their desire to exert power *over* you.

What Workplace Bullies Want to Achieve

Workplace bullies want to use behaviour which results in you experiencing:

- Lowered self-esteem and reduced self-confidence.

- Difficulty performing to your usual standard.

- Self-doubt as you or your co-workers question your commitment or your ability to perform.

- Confusion as your colleagues and co-workers observe what is happening to you but neither intervene nor offer you active support, either at the time of an attack or subsequently, often because they are afraid they will be targeted if they do.

Each bully has their own specific 'reasons' for wanting to use behaviour which they hope will achieve these aims. None of these 'reasons' is justifiable. Here are three common contexts for a campaign of workplace bullying:

- The bully decides to create fog around the fact that they are under-performing. They don't want to work hard to learn the skills, technical knowledge and personal attributes which would result in them performing better. Instead, they decide to undermine and reduce *you* to take the focus off themselves and their own shortcomings.

- The bully decides, rightly or wrongly, that they are already failing at their key performance indicators, or they are likely to fail in the near future. The thought of failure is so awful that they cannot face it. Instead of working hard to up their performance and succeed, they decide to create a scapegoat in you to deflect attention away from themselves and, if possible, start to blame you for some part in their under-performance.

- The bully wants to make sure that you, someone whom they think of as more talented or skilful than themselves, are pegged back a few notches so you don't perform better than them and show them up. In this case, a combination of fear, envy and jealousy drives them to use bullying behaviour in a misguided attempt to eliminate someone they regard as a competitor.

In each of these scenarios the bully resorts to tactics which injure you as an alternative to developing the emotional maturity, people-handling skills and technical knowledge they need to perform effectively. They use their time, energy and inner resources to originate and execute a campaign aimed at undermining you personally and professionally in the hope that, somehow, they will feel better about themselves as a result. But this flawed strategy doesn't work and the bully remains in urgent need of using their time, energy and inner resources to address the issues which sit with them. So, let's now take a deeper look at the role which envy and jealousy can play in a campaign of workplace bullying.

The Role of Jealousy and Envy in Workplace Bullying

Some workplace bullies feel jealousy towards the person they target. Some are envious of them. Others again feel both impulses. What is the difference?

My definition of envy as it relates to workplace bullying is that the bully wants to *take the good that you have earned* - your reputation, personal qualities, learned skills and/or your organisational status and rewards - and *acquire them for themselves.*

My definition of jealousy as it relates to workplace bullying is: the bully wants to *destroy the good that you have earned* - your reputation, your personal qualities, your learned skills and/or your organisational status and rewards - *to prevent you from having them.*

In either of these two cases, the person using bullying behaviour wrongly assumes that, should they succeed and reduce you or your influence, somehow their working life will be better for your defeat. In my experience, this is rarely the case. In most cases, the use of these tactics sets up cycles of relating which work against the best interests of the bully, who loses influence, respect and goodwill as a result of using egregious aggression at work. The outcome of their behaviour is that their colleagues and co-workers learn to fear them, feel intimidated when they are around them, don't volunteer information or opinion to them, and cut them out of information giving and decision-making loops whenever they can. The bully becomes isolated and loses influence. But, more importantly for our purposes here, the people they target can be left devastated by the experience of feeling unsafe and unable to protect themselves from attack in their workplace.

Consider the following short examples:

- A technically proficient but inter-personally awkward lawyer in a small firm hires a newly qualified associate to work alongside her. The associate quickly establishes liking and respect among her colleagues who appreciate her ready ability to connect with them, her desire to work hard, and her intelligence. The technically-minded lawyer to whom the associate reports, notices the rising popularity of the young lawyer and starts to fear for her reputation and standing in the firm. She doesn't like the competition which she decides her underling represents. Instead of working hard to develop the people-handling skills and ability to create trust which comes so naturally to her younger colleague, she becomes jealous and envious of her. She embarks on a subtle, covert campaign of workplace bullying designed to undermine her credibility and take the credit for the associate's work.

- A head librarian in large city library becomes disillusioned that his years of loyal service have not brought him the satisfaction and fulfilment he expected. He becomes bitter and disappointed, slipshod in his work and is rude to his members of staff. He feels jealous towards what he sees as the carefree, devil-may-care attitude of the more junior members of staff and embarks on a campaign of verbal bullying to cut them down to size.

In each of these short examples the central character allows their jealousy or envy to cloud their judgement. Rather than work hard to learn the skills they need, or to address their disappointment with their life choices, each character channels their energy into bullying and undermining their colleagues. These are deeply misguided choices to make.

| **Envy and jealousy are often factors in workplace bullying.** |

Behaviours Often Used By Workplace Bullies

Let's now examine the range of tactics which workplace bullies employ. Each bully will use behaviour which is individual to them so the list below is not exhaustive, but it's a good place to start. You might want to tick the boxes next to the behaviours which you have experienced.

Firstly, consider occasions when the person bullying you talks about you behind your back, when you are not there to defend yourself, so they can unjustly criticise you, your work or your performance. They might:

☐   Exaggerate an error or a misjudgement you have made, so that they can drop the thought into the minds of those nearby that you are not up to your job.

☐   Lie about you, making up errors or mistakes which they say you have made so that they can question your performance or character, however subtly or blatantly they may do so.

☐   Take a fact about you (such as you were in a meeting with so-and-so the other day) and dress it up in fabrications and slander to injure your reputation and credibility (such as implying you were unprepared for the meeting or said something stupid at it).

☐   Take a fact about you and dress it up in a web of deceit to shift blame from their error or wrongdoing and place it with you (such as the bully sends the wrong consignment to a customer with whom you both work but, instead of holding their hands up and learning from their mistake, decides to tell other people it was your fault).

Secondly, consider occasions when the bully targets your performance because they know you are conscientious and that doing a good job is an important component of your self-esteem. They might:

☐ Unfairly criticise your work to your face and to other people, regularly pointing out what they consider to be errors, inefficiencies or deficiencies in the way you carry out your duties: they do this to undermine your confidence, not because they want to help you improve.

☐ Make sure you are assigned too much work to be comfortably completed by a specified deadline: they do this to set you up to fail at an important task, not because they think you will thrive under the challenge.

☐ Deliberately avoid telling you important information, or withhold vital data from you, so that you cannot complete your work to the required standard or on time: they do this to make sure you fail at the task so they can subsequently criticise you privately or publically for under-performing.

☐ Listen to and respond positively to all the points made by colleagues at meetings which you attend, but ignore, talk over or disagree with all the points you make at the same meeting: they do this to undermine and de-stabilise you in front of your co-workers.

Thirdly, consider occasions when the bully uses direct verbal and/or non-verbal aggression when they talk to you. They might:

☐ Clench their fists when looking at you, roll their eyes when you enter the room or tut when you speak at a meeting.

☐ Come into your office, stand in front of you or your desk with their feet planted firmly on the ground, and glare at you.

☐ Whisper confidentially to the person standing or sitting next to them, while maintaining eye contact with you, to imply that they are speaking unfavourably about you (which they might be).

☐ Stomp up to you in a corridor, using their physicality to convey contempt and aggression for you, and speak to you in an openly angry and disrespectful way.

Fourthly, consider occasions when the bully employs practical methods to unsettle and offend you. They might:

☐ Go into your office without your permission when you are not there and move items around on your desk.

☐ Send offensive or upsetting text messages, voice messages or emails to you.

☐ Send offensive email messages from your account to someone else, making it look like you sent them.

☐ Hide paperwork or files you are working on to prevent you from completing tasks on time or to require you to re-do work you have already finished and subsequently cannot find.

In each of these instances, the bully employs behaviour which they think will:

• Undermine your self-esteem.

• Cause you to doubt yourself.

• Leave you feeling confused and on the back foot.

• Reduce your ability to do your job well.

• Injure your reputation.

• Result in colleagues and co-workers questioning your commitment or your skills.

• Drop the thought into your colleagues' and co-workers' minds that you are not up to it, or not as good as they previously thought.

• Reduce your belief in your own competence.

My goal when working with a client, and my goal for you as you read this book, is that you more quickly:

- Recognise a bullying tactic as exactly that: a tactic designed to undermine you.

- Mentally prepare to counter that tactic with an effective response: to send the bully the message that they will not have it all their own way.

- Regain your balance and poise: letting the bully know that you have got the measure of them in that encounter.

- Retain control and influence in the interaction: so you don't fall into self-defeating or toxic thinking, and subsequently waste precious energy worrying about what might happen during your next encounter with the person bullying you.

- De-toxify from workplace bullying experiences: gain a new and healing perspective on your experience and move on from it feeling confident that you can handle similar behaviour effectively in the future.

In order to achieve these aims, you need to understand more about the bullying dynamic which the person targeting you wants to create in their relationship with you. So, let's examine the bullying dynamic in more detail.

What is The Bullying Dynamic?

At the heart of a workplace bullying relationship is the bullying dynamic: the patterns of behaviour which are set up between you and the bully which keep you on the back foot and keep the bully in charge of the interactions between you.

The workplace bully wants to create this bullying dynamic so that they can intimidate you, and control your behaviour to some extent. But the important thing to realise is that when caught up in a bullying dynamic you have much more room for manoeuvre, and much more influence, than you realise. If you are being bullied right now, it may not *feel* like that at all. You may think that the bully has all the power, especially if they are also your boss or an important client who brings income into your organisation or an important fee earner for your employer. You may think that your choices at the time of an attack are very limited indeed, and that the best thing you can do is limit your exposure to the bully as much as possible, get interactions with them over with a quickly as possible, and keep away from them.

All of these strategies have their place, and at key moments they may be very wise strategies to use so that you can create much-needed space and time to recover while you are still at work. But they are helpful strategies to use in the short term only. They won't change the character of the dynamic that is evolving between you and the person bullying you. To do this, you need to realise that there are additional mental, behavioural and verbal options available to you in addition to those you are currently utilising. And that exercising those options simply and straightforwardly will assist you to preserve some or all of your personal power, resist the bully effectively, *and* change the character of the dynamic between you so it works more in your favour.

This *is* true. Even if you find it hard to believe right now.

Think about it. You may not have as much organisational status or informal influence as the person bullying you – although some of you will - but you *do* have as much personal power. Remember that by personal power I am referring to your right to choose how you behave, what you think, what you say and what values matter to you. And the judicious use of your personal power *at the time of an attack* will influence the way the rest of the interaction between you and the bully plays out, and it will result in the subsequent behaviour of the bully changing.

> **You have more influence in a bullying dynamic than you realise.**

Consider the following fictional but realistic case study which illustrates this dynamic.

Case Study 1: Personal Power

A shop worker in the lighting department in a busy high street store is subject to workplace bullying from her manager. Although she does not work with him every day, and indeed he is not based in the same building as her, the manager does come to her store three to four times a week. During these visits he makes a point of coming to the lighting department in order to bully her.

Over the four weeks that she has been subject to bullying behaviour the shop worker has experienced growing anxiety, poor quality sleep, reduced appetite and, recently, reluctance to leave the house to travel to work. Her boss's attacks are random. Sometimes he interacts with her without using coercion, a demeaning tone or an aggressive stance and is superficially pleasant to her. But, on other occasions, he employs all of these bullying tactics, sometimes simultaneously. The fact that she cannot predict when he might be 'nice' and when he might be bullying adds to her confusion, her distress and her self-doubt.

The manager makes a point of attacking his employee when she is working alone, stocking shelves or handling paperwork at her console. Should another colleague be within ear-shot, he is scrupulously pleasant if a little patronising and doesn't employ bullying methods at all. The shop worker starts to wonder whether, since he can be 'nice' and isn't always aggressive, the fault actually lies with her, and it is in fact *she* who is getting things out of proportion in thinking unkind thoughts about *him*.

The pattern of behaviour which has evolved between them plays right into the hands of the bullying manager. He approaches his employee when she is absorbed in her work, and alone. Without preamble, and using a cutting and cold tone, he says: 'Where are you with that work I gave you?' He doesn't specify what work he is referring to, and is quite aware that he hasn't delegated any tasks to her that day. The tone he uses – harsh, unkind, hurtful – creates confusion in the conscientious shop worker as she tries to make sense of the aggression she has just received. His question is unsettling for her, because while it could be taken as an innocent comment without an agenda behind it, the tone is one of insidiousness and innuendo. The combination of an apparently above-board question about her work from her manager, uttered in a tone which is insinuating and sinister, confuses the shop worker and causes her to doubt herself.

At the time of each attack the shop worker reels internally as she tries to understand what she might have done to provoke so much verbal aggression and unreasonable behaviour from her boss. She is shocked into silence as she struggles to find a logical answer to what he has just said to her. She remains vulnerable throughout the entire interaction, literally and metaphorically on the back foot, because she doesn't know what to say or do to protect herself. She doesn't move because the shock renders her immobile. Her mind goes blank and when she tries to find a logical and reasonable response to aggression which is groundless and overwhelming, she cannot find anything to say.

Following a particularly nasty verbal assault in which the boss implied that she might be stealing from the till and he was going to watch her every move, the shop worker – an honest and hardworking woman – decides that she has to find something to say to him the next time she sees him. This is a very difficult thing for her to do as it involves her going onto the front foot, deciding to confront her accuser, and (in her mind) risking an even worse response from him. But she simply cannot allow herself to be accused of stealing when she has never had the thought, and she decides to act.

That evening she plans what she wants to say. She writes it down. She rehearses the wording in front of a mirror. She practises what she will say until she knows the wording by heart. This is important to her. She wants all her energy to be available to her when she confronts her manager. She wants to be present to the interaction between them rather than worrying about what she will say.

Back at work, she waits for the next time he walks into the department and summons all her courage. She takes a deep breath and, before he has had time to scan the shelves to locate her, she walks towards him with her head held high and her shoulders back. She walks straight towards him and when she is a few feet from him but still walking she starts to speak. She tells him in level, respectful but clear tones, that the last time he spoke to her she heard him imply that she might be stealing from the till. She tells him that he must be joking, that she has never had the thought and that if he persists in making unfounded accusations she will take things further. She quite deliberately doesn't say in what way she will take things further. She maintains level eye contact with him throughout, doesn't waver in her intention to put the issues back to him, and watches his face to see how he will react.

The bullying manager is initially thrown by the combination of quiet dignity and clear certainty demonstrated by the shop worker. She does not display any of the anxiety or timidity which had made her an easy target, and he is momentarily thrown. But he quickly recovers his composure. He squares his jaw and tells her that she must have misunderstood him. Adopting a patronising, snide and cutting tone he starts to tell her that he is really too busy to talk to her and has more important things to do when she interrupts him and speaks again.

She says that yes she *must* have misunderstood him, because he couldn't possibly have made an unfounded accusation of theft against a worker with ten years' service, when there is no evidence to back up the accusation. She then tells him that they both know she hasn't stolen money from the till. She looks him straight in the eye as she says this.

The manager swallows and, after a short pause in which he looks nonplussed, he moves away without saying anything else. The shop worker returns to the aisle where she was working and gets on with her work. She keeps an eye on the manager, observes him speaking to a number of her colleagues, and to several customers, and then watches him as he walks out of the department.

Analysing the Dynamics in Case Study 1: Personal Power

What does the shop worker's courage tell us about the nature of the bullying dynamic that had evolved between her and her manager? And what does it tell us about why her carefully-crafted confrontation results in her manager simply walking away on this occasion?

Firstly, we can say that the manager demonstrates considerable cowardice in his choice of target. He selects a shop worker over whom he has organisational authority and who largely carries out her duties alone. He deliberately confuses her by sometimes being 'nice' and other times being bullying, which results in the shop worker not knowing what to expect from any interaction with him. Her confusion is so great that she actually begins to think it might be her that is at fault, and not him. Her good nature results in her wondering whether *she* isn't actually being unfair to *him*.

Secondly, we can say that her shock and distress at being targeted in this random fashion results in her being floored at the time of each attack. She simply cannot find anything to say back to him and she remains largely silent and still while he bullies her. A pattern of behaviour develops between them whereby:

- He says something aggressive, nasty or untrue.

- She is shocked into silence.

- As she recovers sufficiently to *want* to say something back to him, her mind is blank and she can't find any logical response to his unwarranted criticism and malice.

- She remains silent and still throughout the remainder of the encounter, enabling him to add another offensive comment if he wishes before walking away.

However, when he pushes her too far and attacks her integrity and honesty as a person and as an employee, she pushes back. She plans her confrontation carefully, rehearses what she wants to say. She chooses her moment, takes a deep breath and engages him. Her physical demeanour is one of self-confidence. She stands tall. She holds her head high. She looks him in the eye as she approaches him, and maintains level eye contact with him as she addresses him.

He is now on the back foot and the dynamic of the interaction is quite different. This time:

- She is in charge and completes what she has planned to say without being interrupted.

- He is initially wrong footed and has to listen to her clear, calm and dignified delivery as she tells him that she has not stolen anything and that it would not occur to her to do so.

- He hears her self-confidence and is silenced by it.

- However, he does quite quickly regain his composure. He finds his voice and begins to tell her that she has misunderstood him. He then tries to go onto the front foot and regain control by belittling her. But when he starts to tell her that he has more important things to do than talk to her he is further surprised when she interrupts him – something she has not done before – and puts him into a clever double bind from which he cannot easily escape.

- She tells him that she *must* have misunderstood him and that he *could not possibly* have implied she would steal from her employer. Then she tells him that *they both know* she hasn't stolen anything from the till. This is a smart thing to do, as using this tactic makes it quite clear that she and she alone reserves the right to choose what she believes about herself and what her values are – and tells him that she is quite clear that he is lying and that *she knows he knows he is lying.*

- The manager is defeated by her combination of self-assurance and clarity that she is not, and could never be, a thief. And by her view that she knows that he knows that too. His attempt to cause her to doubt her integrity and truthfulness completely backfire on him as she turns the table on him by her decision to confront him.

- To save face he walks away from her, leaving the department shortly afterwards.

- This time she has won. In the future he may well be tempted to try to bully her again. But, if she has observed what happened this time round carefully enough, the shop worker will realise that this bully only bullies people who doubt themselves, who don't know how to push back, and who are unable to find anything to say at the time of an attack. He will think twice about bullying her again because he now knows that when she puts her mind to it she does not fall into any of these categories. The manager now knows that she can defend herself very ably by putting the issues back to him; and the shop worker now realises that this bully *only uses the room which she gives to him,* and that when she cuts down that room for manoeuvre he stops bullying her.

Let's explore these issues further in a separate, shorter example.

Exploring the Bullying Dynamic

- An HR advisor is designing a recruitment process for one of her colleagues, a trading floor head in an investment bank. The HR advisor's role involves identifying core competencies, working with selected head-hunting firms to identify suitable candidates, and recruiting a capable, robust trader to join the trading floor head's team by the end of the quarter. The trading floor head routinely bullies everyone in his team. From his initial meeting with the HR advisor, he bullies her too. During every telephone call and one-to-one meeting between them, the trading floor head employs the tactic of making humiliating and undermining comments to the HR advisor in an attempt to injure her self-esteem and reduce her confidence in her own abilities. The HR advisor works very hard on the project. Well aware of the trading floor head's fearsome reputation, she endeavours to make swift progress. Nonetheless, her efforts at pre-empting his irritable and impatient nature don't work, and he routinely subjects her to ridicule. His belittling questions and comments are usually broached in a tone of withering contempt, and include: 'Are you going to do anything useful in relation to this simple task?' or 'I asked you to perform a simple set of duties. I can see no signs of progress. Are you actually awake?' On each occasion that he speaks to her in this way, the HR advisor adopts a silent and still demeanour, in the hope of sending the message to her assailant that she is unperturbed by his tactics. However, her apparent nonchalance to his rebukes does not result in him desisting, and the HR advisor becomes fed up at being attacked by an internal client on whose behalf she is working hard.

Late on the afternoon before she is due to meet the first head-hunter, she receives a call while she is working at her desk. She picks up the call, gives her name and says: 'How can I help?' Without introducing himself or saying hello, the trading floor head bluntly informs her: 'Your dull and unimaginative approach to a simple project isn't good enough. Don't bother to attend the meeting with the head-hunter tomorrow. I'll go myself.' In the silence that follows, the HR advisor takes a deep breath. Aware that this is a pivotal moment in their relationship, and one she cannot afford to mishandle, she summons up her courage. Using a firm and even tone, she says: 'You have delegated a task to me, and I am working on it. You now need to place your reservations to one side and trust me to do my job. You can, of course attend the meeting with the head-hunter tomorrow, but I will also be there, as there are a number of important points I want to put to the head-hunter.' She then politely reminds the trading floor head of the time of the meeting and hangs up.

In this example, a bullying trading floor head uses a combination of verbal hostility and undermining remarks to unsettle his HR advisor. He does this in the expectation that she will not know how to defend herself, will believe some or all of his comments, and will start to doubt her own competence. His way will then be clear to maintain a bullying dynamic between them. Initially, this is exactly what happens. Her passivity in the face of his aggression enables him to continue with his tactics unopposed.

The trading floor head makes aggressive comments, and asks crudely-framed questions, each of which is an attempt to cause the HR advisor to doubt herself. Even though she is well aware of his reputation, and expects him to be a difficult customer, she is unable to handle his mixture of acerbic questions and blatant aggression. So thrown is she by his bullying, that she allows each comment or question to go unchallenged. In the silence which follows each of his attacks, she goes onto the back foot and is unable to counter the attack with a response, inadvertently encouraging him to continue with his verbal assaults whenever he is next minded to do so. It is only when he decides to take over her role, and replace her at the meeting she has arranged with one of the head-hunters, that she decides to draw the line. She does so very effectively. Her carefully-crafted response to his aggression simultaneously:

- Asserts her right to do her job, her way, whether he likes it or not.

- Makes it clear that the trading floor head will not be able to push her out of her own meeting.

- Positions herself as the expert on matters of recruitment, and the best person to discuss them with the head-hunter.

- Avoids antagonising him by suggesting that he should not attend the meeting, and should leave it to her.

- Reminds him of the time of the meeting, to make it clear to him that she retains ownership of the meeting, and that she knows what she is doing.

She will need to handle that meeting deftly, maintaining her more assertive and self-confident stance throughout, and during all her subsequent encounters with the trading floor head. At no point should she give her power back to him by:

- Mentally going onto the back foot again.

- Remaining silent while he bullies her.

- Relaxing her demeanour when she meets him, in the assumption that, since she has got the measure of him, he will cease bullying her.

- Failing to portray herself as proactive, confident and on top of her work.

The HR advisor has a tough job on her hands if she is to continue to serve the trading floor head as well as she would like. But she has learned that by demonstrating confidence in her own abilities, especially in the moment of an attack, she goes a long way towards reversing the bullying dynamic between them, and making it much more challenging for him to target her.

Summary of the Key Points from the Chapter

Workplace bullies want to intimidate you. They want a combination of your fear and their aggression to render you powerless at the time of an attack. The bullying dynamic they want to create is therefore about:

- The intimidating behaviour they employ with you.

- How you react outwardly to that hostility at the time of the attack.

- The patterns of behaviour that become the norm between you during the period of their campaign against you.

The bully wants you to:

- Feel intimidated and anxious.

- Decide not to fight back either because you are too afraid to or because you don't know how to do so effectively.

- Outwardly comply with what they want so they remain in control of the encounter between you.

And, if you are caught up in a bullying dynamic, it can seem as if the best thing to do is not to fight back and to simply try and get the encounter over with quickly.

But, you have more influence in the interaction between you and the bully than you think. Your ability to decide for yourself what you will think, say and do at the time of an attack – and your decision about your values – will to some extent influence the patterns of behaviour that play out between you and the bully during that interaction. Calling on your personal power – your right to decide who you are and how you will behave – will impact the dynamic between you from the moment you speak out onwards.

Even though the bully is unlikely to let you know it, your decision to put the issues back to them will result in their subsequent behaviour altering. Some bullies only use the room for manoeuvre you inadvertently give them. Cutting down this room for manoeuvre cuts down their options for bullying you and enables you to regain some measure of control.

So - and this is the crucial thing - the power you have in any abusive situation in the workplace is three-fold. It is the power to:

- Decide for yourself what is true about you and what you believe.

- Decide for yourself what you will say and do at the time of an attack.

- Choose how you will behave, including how you will carry out your duties and perform your job.

Using your personal power wisely at the time of an attack will be self-preserving and self-protective for you. Subsequent chapters of this book will help you develop further skills in identifying the options and choices you have in the moment of an attack: options and choices which, if you exercise them wisely, will also be both self-protective and self-preserving for you.

Questions for You to Consider

Having considered the material in this chapter you might now want to apply it to your own experience by answering the questions below. You can jot down your answer to each question in the space below it.

1. To what extent do you think you are subject to bullying behaviour at work?

2. Who is bullying you? In what situations do they choose to attack you?

3. What behaviour and tactics does this person employ to bully you?

4. How do you typically respond at the time of an attack?

5. How would you describe the bullying dynamic that has evolved between you and the bully?

Next Chapter

Chapter 3 will examine the negative impact your experiences of workplace bullying may have had on your self-image. It discusses the sometimes catastrophic effect bullying can have on what you think about yourself, what you believe about yourself, what you feel, and how you behave.

Chapter 3
The Impact of Workplace Bullying

Self-Defeating Thoughts and Toxic Beliefs

The Devastating Effects of Workplace Bullying

If you have first-hand experiences of being bullied at work, you will know that the consequences can affect every area of your life. An experience of workplace bullying can be devastating. It can affect you psychologically, emotionally and physically. It can result in the quality of your work reducing as your energy goes inward to deal with the abusive behaviour you are subject to. It means that, as your energy is taken up dealing with trauma, you start to do things differently: at work, with your family, with your friends. You respond differently. You think differently. You're not as enthusiastic as usual or as well presented. You don't sleep as well and your appetite may reduce or increase. Your closest colleagues may well recognise that you are struggling. Some of them may want to support you, others won't know how to. It is likely that at some point in an on-going situation of abuse your performance will be impacted and you will no longer be able to produce the quality of work you are known for.

Being subject to workplace bullying can quite literally paralyse you. You may have worked alongside the person who bullied you for weeks, months or years before they attacked you. Or they might have subjected you to aggression the first time they worked with you. You may be so shocked by the behaviour you have experienced that you wonder if you have actually done something wrong, something sufficiently terrible to justify the attack on you. Some of you have expended much energy and internal resources forensically going through what you said or did prior to a particular attack trying to account for why it occurred. You think you must have said something or done something to provoke the attack, and want to know what it was so you can avoid doing it again.

On occasion, you might identify a small mistake or an error of judgement, leading you to wonder if you have underestimated the importance of the slip-up and *that* is reason you were subject to aggression. But, most of the time you cannot find anything that you have mishandled, overlooked or done poorly. And yet your self-doubt and confusion persist as you keep returning to the thought that you *must* have done *something* to at least provide a context for the attack on you. And every time you have that thought, there is an escalation of the spiral of worry about what will happen the next time you encounter the bully.

This chapter will examine the range of consequences that you may recognise in your working and private life as a result of being subject to workplace bullying. It will explore how your experience of being bullied might have affected you, identify a range of changes you may have made to help you cope with your experience of being bullied, and highlight the potentially adverse impact of bullying behaviour on what you think, what you feel, and what you believe about yourself.

Toxic Shame: Blaming Yourself

Many people who have been bullied at work blame themselves. They feel shame at being targeted. They think that in some way they must be responsible for the bully's use of aggressive, coercive behaviour towards them. They try and help the bully see the error of their ways. They try to change the bully.

Assuming responsibility for the bully's decision to target you means that you burden yourself with a load you cannot be responsible for - the actions of the bully – while you are also struggling to handle the trauma of being targeted. The mental slide into self-blame and trying to change the bully can greatly add to your suffering and confusion.

Hear this. You are not to blame for the actions of the bully. They and they alone chose to target you, to use aggression towards you in your workplace, and to square this approach with their conscience. These issues sit with them. Your responsibility is to learn to protect yourself at the time of an attack.

Any confusion or self-doubt you have about this issue may result in you adopting any or all of the following ineffective strategies when in an encounter with the bully:

- Appealing to the bully's 'better nature': a strategy which pre-supposes that the bully possesses a measure of goodwill and that you can somehow induce them to extend it to you.

- Trying to reason with the bully: which pre-supposes that a logical argument will prove influential with a person whose use of angry emotion at work suggests that they are unlikely to be persuaded by rational argument.

- Trying to appease them: which pre-supposes that the bully is amenable to being mollified and soothed, and that if you try hard enough you will work out how to do this effectively.

- Feeling sorry for the bully: which pre-supposes that the bully is somehow being unfairly treated and deserving of sympathy, when it is actually *they* who are choosing to mistreat *you*, and *you* who are deserving of empathy for being targeted by *them*.

None of these strategies is in your best interests. Each of them is based on the assumption that you have done something wrong which has caused their aggression and that there is something you can do differently which will:

- Prevent the bully from being aggressive.

- Reduce the level of their aggression towards you.

- Cause them to change their minds entirely about bullying you.

The starting point for using effective strategies is not thinking that you are responsible for the actions or the feelings of someone acting abusively towards you. The starting point is to hold that person accountable for what they are saying and doing at the time of an attack, and to use self-protective and self-preserving behaviour while simultaneously putting the issues back to them. Subsequent chapters in this book will show you exactly how to do this.

It is really important that you get this: you are not the cause of the aggression used by the bully. Even if your performance is not up to scratch, you still have done nothing to warrant the aggression being used against you. Effective management and bullying are two entirely different things. Many workplace bullies will do everything they can to blame you for how they feel, to make you 'the problem' they complain about, and to single you out for personalised enmity. But these are their decisions and their responsibility alone, and they are not the behaviours used by effective managers, even those taxed by how to coach an underperformer to perform better.

You did not provoke the attack on you and you do not deserve to be targeted.

The default position of a bully is to use aggression with several, all or selected targets at work. And, if you are one of those targets, you have not done anything to justify the aggression you are subject to. It may help to think in the following terms. Imagine a continuum which describes the values that people at work use when relating to colleagues and co-workers. At one end of the continuum is a default pattern of relating that is about wanting to promote collaborative connections based on mutuality, goodwill, collegiality and partnership. At the other end of the continuum is a default pattern of relating that is about wanting to promote connections based on competition, hostility, manipulation and control. There are many possible points in between these two extremes. Bullies operate at one end of this spectrum. This is their choice. It is their default setting. It is not something the target can possibly provoke. It is a long-standing, pre-existing way of doing things that is likely to be a fundamentally different perspective from those they target.

With that core truth in mind, let's examine some of the behaviour you might be using at the time of an attack which, though well-intentioned, isn't in your best interests. Two of the most common ineffective responses to workplace bullying are to:

- Avoid confronting the bully's use of aggression at work.

And to:

- Comply with the bully's wishes at the time of an attack.

Both of these patterns of behaviour are understandable. But neither of them is a wise choice of response to bullying in the long run.

Avoiding: A Common Response to Workplace Bullying

Avoiding a workplace bully is due to the desire to avoid feeling the potentially overwhelming levels of anxiety and fear which may result on occasions when you see, speak to or have an encounter with the bully. If you relate to this description, you may feel paralysed and disabled when in the presence of the person targeting you. To avoid feeling this toxic mixture of incapacity and fear you avoid situations where it is likely you will encounter the bully and, when subject to attack from them, or subsequent to an attack from them, you avoid confronting their bullying behaviour. Social embarrassment is also a factor. You want to avoid an upsetting scene playing out in front of more junior staff, people who report to you or your bosses.

With great compassion, you really need to hear this: you probably avoid confronting because you don't know how to confront safely. But every time you avoid, you give away your power. Every time you go out of your way to avoid a meeting with the person bullying you and every time you avoid confronting their use of abusive behaviour towards you, you undermine your own cause. Every time you let the bully's aggressive behaviour go unchallenged, you send them the message that they can continue to attack you as and when they want to, and you will not put up a stop sign.

For many of you, fear of confronting the bully is actually a fear that, if you do confront them, they will retaliate more powerfully than previously and damage you irreparably or, worse, destroy you. If you are struggling with the fear of being damaged or destroyed I want to extend a message of hope. Judicious use of the tactics and strategies in this book will enable you to challenge the bully safely and effectively at the time of an attack, and will mean that you are able to retain some or all of your power when you are in an abusive encounter with them.

> **Every time you avoid you give away your power.**

Complying: A Second Common Response to Workplace Bullying

The second of the two most common ineffective responses to workplace bullying is complying. In the context of workplace bullying, I think of complying as being the desire to submit as a strategy for getting through a challenging encounter with the bully. If this resonates with you, you may feel that the only way to preserve even a slender thread of connection between yourself and the bully is to do what they want. Your desire to maintain some form of relationship with that person is understandable. You work with them. You may have a closely-structured working relationship with them. Your roles may be such that you cannot achieve your key performance indicators without working with them to some degree. The person targeting you may have greater organisation influence than you and could adversely affect your reputation among other senior managers or even negatively impact your career path. There may be many reasons why maintaining some form of connection with the bully is desirable for you.

Your desire to keep some form of connection between you is understandable. But let's make a distinction between:

- The intention to preserve a working relationship with a non-bullying, but challenging, colleague.

And:

- The strategy of compliance or submission towards a workplace bully.

The former makes complete sense, no matter how difficult it may be in practice. The latter isn't wise.

When working alongside a workplace bully, compliance works against your best interests. The only form of connection this strategy preserves with your bullying co-worker is one predicated on them using coercion and fear to control you. Every time you submit, you give away your power. Every time you do what the bully wants without exercising your right to choose how you behave and how you carry out your role, you let them know that they are in sole charge of the encounter, and that their aggression controls your behaviour to some extent. They have all the encouragement they need to continue to use their intimidating tactics.

Your bullying colleague or co-worker is a dangerous person to want to preserve connection with. It would be much safer for you in the long run to learn how to handle them effectively at the time of an attack.

The Consequences of Avoiding and Complying

Patterns of avoidant and compliant behaviour play straight into the hands of the person targeting you. Consider the following diagram which illustrates how these two patterns of behaviour play out following an incident of workplace bullying.

Read the following diagram in a clockwise direction starting with the circle at 12 o'clock:

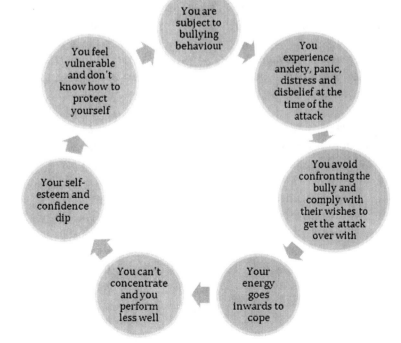

Diagram 1: Avoiding and complying: common reactions to workplace bullying

Let's see how patterns of avoiding and complying play out between a main character and the person bullying them in three short examples.

- A conscientious healthcare worker is subject to workplace bullying from his peer. The two healthcare workers share an office and work on jointly-structured tasks, analysing lab results for acute in-patients. The bullying peer is the more robust and forthright of the two characters. She is also cutting, nasty and snide. In order to cope with the pressure he feels under at being regularly humiliated in his own office, the conscientious healthcare worker starts to come in earlier and leave later, using the hospital's flexi-time arrangements to his advantage. He thinks that reducing the time he is in their shared office will cut down the opportunity his peer has to attack him. While it is true that he spends a smaller proportion of each day in her presence, this strategy does not protect him in the long run. She continues to bully him, albeit during a shorter portion of the day. As his energy goes inwards to cope with the continued assaults on him, so his work quality starts to reduce and he begins to make mistakes. His bullying colleague takes advantage of his cowed demeanour and increased vulnerability. She suggests to him that he isn't up to the job any longer and ought to quit before he makes an error which results in serious harm to a patient. The conscientious peer continues to try and get through the day as best he can but doesn't confront his peer's bullying.

- An energetic and outgoing junior accountant is subject to workplace bullying from his manager. In order to cope with the attacks on him, he starts and ends each day in the gym, regularly arriving for work later than he usually would. He makes a point of booking a private meeting room for two hours a day so he can get away from his manager whose office is next door to his. When he is in the meeting room he switches off his mobile phone. This strategy does afford him some respite from the bullying he is subject to, but it also means that his other colleagues and some of his clients cannot get hold of him as easily as they used to do. His manager overhears two colleagues remark innocently that they don't know where the junior accountant gets to these days. The manager takes advantage of the situation by suggesting to the partner-in-charge that the junior accountant hides away in a meeting room all day because he is out of his depth, struggling with the work and not up to the cut and thrust of life in the firm. The junior accountant continues to employ the strategy of avoidance and does not confront his manager's bullying behaviour, unaware that his reputation has just taken a hit.

- A warm and popular junior school teacher is subject to workplace bullying from an envious school secretary. Unable to cope with the emotional overwhelm she experiences at being targeted by a co-worker she likes, the teacher starts to withdraw from social situations in the school. She doesn't go to the staff room at break time and starts to eat her lunch in her car, which she drives out of the school gates and parks in a nearby street. The teacher becomes more rigid and aloof with the children in her class and, when she is in a meeting with teaching colleagues or her head of department, seems absent-minded and distracted. The teacher worries that she isn't the person she used to be, but doesn't know what to do to regain her enjoyment of her job or her life. The school secretary watches these developments with interest and waits for the opportunity to tell selected colleagues that she thinks the teacher looks peaky and needs to take a break. The teacher continues to avoid her colleagues as much as possible and doesn't confront the school secretary. Her colleagues start to question her commitment behind her back.

In each of these short examples, the target recognises that they are subject to unreasonable and punishing behaviour and makes sensible changes designed to keep them apart from the person bullying them. They succeed in creating space for themselves while they are at work and this helps them cope with what is happening to them to some degree. But in all three cases the target is still subject to bullying behaviour, albeit less frequently, and they are not fully protected from further attack. Their energy continues to go inwards to help them cope, and as their work standards and demeanour alter, they become vulnerable to being misinterpreted by colleagues who are sufficiently removed from the situation that they are not aware of the bullying.

Confronting Your Powerlessness and Toxic Thoughts

Some of the most challenging incidents of workplace bullying that my clients have reported to me involved them *feeling powerless to do anything to protect themselves at the time of an attack.* They consequently became *deeply anxious* about what might happen to them during future attacks.

Feelings of powerlessness are highly toxic. They result in you forming faulty beliefs about yourself including believing you are helpless. Believing you are helpless directly leads to further self-defeating thinking which adds to your overwhelm. Sadly, you may continue to mentally beat yourself up even after the bully has left the room, effectively continuing their destructive work for them. Your toxic thinking can end up doing you as much harm – or even more – than the bully's abusive behaviour.

If this description resonates with you then take a deep breath and hear this. You are not helpless. You don't yet know how to protect yourself from workplace bullying but you can learn how to. *It is crucial to realise that your feelings of helplessness are not telling you the truth.* They are reflections of how you feel about yourself because you have been adversely affected by bullying behaviour. When you understand that it cannot possibly be your fault that a bully targeted you, there will be no need to beat yourself up. You can change the patterns of behaviour which currently play out between you and the person bullying you. You can do this, even if you don't yet know how to or don't believe that it is possible. You can handle future attacks more effectively than at present, and you can learn the behavioural strategies which will be self-protective and self-preserving for you should you need them in the future.

Set the intention to re-direct the energy that has been fuelling your self-defeating thoughts. Do it right now! In future you are going to channel this energy into learning how to protect yourself at the time of an attack. You are going to learn to send the bully a powerful message - that you will no longer be an easy target.

Changing the way you handle the bully will change how you feel about them. More importantly, changing the way you handle them will change the way you feel about *yourself.* It will also change what you think about yourself. You will begin to feel more confident and more assertive, and these developments will improve your self-esteem.

The starting point is to tackle your self-defeating thinking and toxic beliefs. You can make a start right now by completing the following exercise.

Exercise 1: Tackling Self-Defeating Thoughts and Toxic Beliefs

The first step in changing the way you think about yourself is to identify the self-defeating thoughts and toxic beliefs which play out in your mind. The following exercise encourages you to identify any self-defeating thoughts or toxic beliefs and replace them with new, more realistic, life-giving thoughts and beliefs.

The exercise starts with five common sets of self-defeating thoughts and toxic beliefs which often play out in the minds of people who have experienced workplace bullying, each of which adds to the overwhelm and despondency in their lives. The examples may or may not apply directly to you, but they ought to help you get started.

Beginning now, and extending over the next few days, monitor the thoughts and beliefs that pop into your head and write them down in the space below. If you need more space you can use the blank page at the back of this book or a separate notebook. Challenge each self-defeating thought or belief. No matter how true it feels to you, take a fresh look at it. Re-assess it. Can you be absolutely certain it is the TRUTH about you? What factual evidence is there is support that thought or belief? What factual evidence is there to challenge it? Just because you think or believe something to be true about you, doesn't necessarily mean it is. There is a world of difference between a thought or belief you entertain which is not actually true, and one that is. Only thoughts and beliefs that are supported by *factual evidence* are actually true. Look for factual evidence to support every thought or belief you generate about yourself. Be open to the possibility that some or all of your thoughts and beliefs are not factual at all, but are a reflection of how you FEEL because you have been bullied.

Having re-evaluated each self-defeating thought or belief, create a new and more life-giving alternative to replace it. Write it down alongside the original in the space below. At the end of the week, look back at what you have written. Commit to re-reading the life-giving thoughts and beliefs every day, so that you don't fall back into your old, self-defeating thinking habits. Whenever an old, self-defeating thought enters your head, commit to writing it down and assessing it for truthfulness.

Self-Defeating Thoughts and Beliefs	Life-Giving Thoughts and Beliefs
1. I am useless!	1. I am competent at many things AND I am having a tough time at the moment
2. I can't handle this	2. I can learn to handle bullying behaviour better than at present
3. I am isolated and alone – no one at work cares what's happening to me	3. I can support myself until I find effective sources of help inside and outside the workplace
4. I can't change, it's too difficult, I don't know where to start	4. I can change – it might take a bit of time and effort, but I can do it
5. I'm not assertive, I never have been	5. Right now I struggle to use assertive behaviour – but I can learn to do so
6. ...	6. ...
7. ...	7. ...
8. ...	8. ...
9. ...	9. ...
10. ...	10. ...

Let's now apply the material from this chapter to a case study.

Case Study 2: Paralysed

A successful fee earner in an IT consultancy firm regularly employs bullying behaviour. He is well known throughout the firm for screaming, shouting, swearing and standing physically close to the colleague he has selected for attack. Having vented his rage in this fashion, he walks away and carries on with his day as if nothing unusual has just happened.

The fee earner has worked for the firm for ten years and brings in more income than any other client-handler in the business. His success as an income generator means that the executives who run the firm turn a blind eye to his appalling behaviour. The fee earner makes a point of addressing only junior members of staff in this outrageous way: members of the human resources department, members of the secretarial pool, or members of the facilities management department who manage the firm's offices. He does not target fellow fee earners, robust technically-minded colleagues, or the heads of any of the firm's departments. He thinks these colleagues would take a dim view of his aggressive tactics should he try and bully them. Instead, the status-conscious and superior fee earner targets members of staff who have no managerial responsibilities, who he thinks are not likely to have much influence outside their own team, and who he thinks of as soft targets.

The fee earner is engaged in a complex project which involves re-designing a number of technology platforms across his key client's premises. His client, the MD of a manufacturing company, is demanding, awkward and uncompromising. As the deadline for phase one of the roll-out draws near, the fee earner's stress levels rise, his tolerance levels diminish and his desire to bully increases.

His anger crystalizes around the issue of the covers for the progress report he has prepared for his client, and specifically centres on the fact that the print media team has yet to send back to him ten glossy report covers with which he intends to bind the document. Annoyed at the delay in receiving the report covers, which were due on his desk two hours ago, the fee earner picks up the telephone on his desk. He rapidly punches out the extension number of the media team helpdesk. He hears the call being picked up and, without waiting for the helpdesk technician to speak, he launches into a diatribe of abuse and criticism.

He tells the hapless helpdesk technician that he is sick and tired of the wasteful inefficiency, crap standards and sloppy work of the media team. He rages at him, telling him that if his report covers are not in his office in precisely five minutes, he'll be coming down to the 'burrow' in which they all work and getting them himself. Then he slams the telephone down and looks at the clock.

Five minutes later, with no report covers on his desk, the fee earner marches out of his office, along the corridor and swiftly descends three flights of stairs. He charges through the door connecting the stairwell with the second floor and heads for the print media team office. As he approaches it, he notices two print media team members chatting companionably outside the door. He brushes them forcibly aside, telling them that they should be working not shirking, and barges his way into the office.

He walks in, quickly assesses that there are five people in the large, open-plan room and walks smartly up to the nearest of them: the team secretary who is standing near the doorway. He puts his face straight into her face, and demands to be directed towards the useless idiot he was unfortunate enough to speak to five minutes ago. The team secretary is so shocked and terrified she nods her head towards the helpdesk technician whose console is a few feet away. The helpdesk technician shrinks back in his chair, immobilised with anxiety and shock, as he prepares to receive another full-on tirade of abuse and fury from the bullying fee earner.

The helpdesk technician is a quiet man, technically excellent with print and media, but not comfortable with confrontation. He remains seated and paralysed during the second it takes for the fee earner to reach his desk. During the verbal abuse that follows, the helpdesk technician simply stares up at the fee earner from behind his desk as the more influential man berates him for being useless at his job, for being lazy, for not being customer focused and for being a waste of space. Satisfied, the fee earner then stomps off without picking up the report covers which are actually by the photocopier ready to be collected.

In the relative calm that follows, the team secretary slowly walks over to the helpdesk technician and touches him lightly on the shoulder. She observes his white face and shocked expression, and says: "Are you all right?"

Analysing the Dynamics in Case Study 2: Paralysed

Let's examine the dynamics at play in this case study in which a helpdesk technician is bullied face-to-face after being subject to bullying over the telephone. Shortly, we will discuss the thoughts, beliefs and feelings that play out in the life of the helpdesk technician. But we will begin by taking a look inside the life of the bullying fee earner.

- Firstly, we can say that the bullying fee earner employs a nasty mixture of status consciousness and rage to subjugate anyone he chooses. He makes it his business to target people with little organisational influence who are unlikely to know how to stand up to someone as senior and influential as him.

- Secondly, he uses the element of surprise to make his attacks all the more vicious and challenging to repel. His initial attack on the helpdesk technician is over the telephone, giving him the option of simply launching into a diatribe of abuse, anonymously and from the comfort of his own office, as soon as the call is picked up. His second attack is delivered in person immediately he enters the print media team office, again giving little or no time for his targets to adjust to his presence in the room and mentally prepare for an attack.

- Thirdly, he knows he will get away with his vicious behaviour – his seniors have turned a blind eye to it for years. With no one to hold him accountable in the hierarchy above him, he simply gives himself free rein to indulge his rage whenever he feels minded to, certain that no one with any organisational clout is likely to confront him.

- Fourthly, because he places his face and body so close to those of the target in the moment of a face-to-face attack, he wants to physically dominate his target. He is a serious adversary and a dangerous foe.

- Fifthly, at no point during the above scenario was the fee earner truly interested in whether he did or did not receive the report covers that day. Instead, he uses the fact that, in his mind at least, the report covers ought to have been delivered to him two hours previously as an excuse to justify his rage. How do we know this? Because when he is in the print media office he does not once ask where the report covers are, or make any attempt to look for them. Had he done so, he would have found them by the photocopier, ready to go. He uses the first attack over the telephone to set up the subsequent face-to-face attack. He does this so he can unleash some of his own pent up anxiety and internal tension. This is an example of a more senior colleague creating a scapegoat out of another more junior colleague so he can 'feel better' and he achieves it without any challenge at all.

Now let's turn to the helpdesk technician and take a look at what is going on inside his life. Firstly, we can say that the helpdesk technician is a quiet and meek man. His nature is reserved and, while excellent at his job technically, he is not fluent verbally and shies away from confrontation. His colleagues respect his knowledge and skills, and regularly look to him for the lead in the office, but they don't know him very well. He comes to work, does his job and goes home again. He doesn't feel particularly valued by his employers in the firm, but he enjoys what he does and that is enough for him.

At the time of the first attack over the telephone, the helpdesk technician is taken completely unawares. In the opening seconds of being yelled at down the phone he is immobilised and unable to speak. He guesses that the person screaming at him is the fee earner whose report covers he has been working on, but he is instantly overwhelmed by the aggression he is subject to. He feels intimidated by the fee earner's seniority in the firm, doesn't know how to stand up to someone who has more organisational influence than him, and someone who is known throughout the firm as a bully who acts with impunity. A combination of him believing himself to be relatively unimportant in the firm and not knowing how to assert himself at the time of either attack make it relatively easy for the practised bully to attack him twice in quick succession. Let's look closely at what happened to identify how these two factors play out during the two separate but connected attacks on him.

The fee earner's initial telephone call takes the helpdesk technician by surprise. As soon as he picks up the telephone receiver, the helpdesk technician is assaulted in a verbal tirade that attacks the standards to which he works along with the work ethic and values of the entire print media team. The fee earner does not introduce himself: he simply rages. He characterises the print media team's office as a 'burrow' and tells the helpdesk technician that if he doesn't get his report covers in five minutes he'll come down and get them himself. He then slams the phone down.

During the entire call, the helpdesk technician does not say one word. The way in which the fee earner sets up the attack – out of the blue, over the phone, without saying who he is – takes the helpdesk technician totally by surprise and renders him speechless. He is completely ambushed. He doesn't manage to find anything to say at the time of the attack, and after it has ceased he is unable to prepare for the second assault which follows. He misses two clear opportunities to act in his own best interests. The first: to protect himself at the time of the telephone attack by either finding something effective to say back to his abuser, or by replacing the receiver to end the encounter. The second: to prepare for the likely second attack about which he has just had warning. When the second face-to-face attack occurs, he then misses a third opportunity to protect himself. He continues to employ avoiding and complying behaviour: he lets the bully have it all his own way unopposed.

We will return to this case study in Chapter 5 to see what steps were open to the helpdesk technician to protect himself on each of three occasions: during the telephone call, in between the telephone call and the face-to-face attack, and during the face-to-face attack. The options available to the helpdesk technician are limited, but he does have some and we will explore them in detail. But for now, let's continue to examine what is going on inside his life that renders him vulnerable to this particularly nasty attack. Let's identify the role that his self-defeating thinking and toxic beliefs play in his paralysis.

The helpdesk technician's paralysis at the time of the attacks on him is partly fuelled by his self-defeating thinking and toxic beliefs. He believes that he is not an important member of staff and that there isn't much he can do to defend himself from a senior figure in the firm who is well known as a bully and who gets away with it. He thinks it is pointless to try and challenge such a powerful adversary, so he doesn't. His thinking about himself, his place in the firm, and the futility of trying to defend himself, creates both paralysis and inertia in him at the time of both attacks. These factors also leave him vulnerable to future attack because he has let the bully know that when he is bullied he simply absorbs punishment compliantly and does nothing to challenge that behaviour. He avoids confronting the bully and sets up a pattern of behaviour in which he remains passive when subject to attack.

Had the helpdesk technician completed Exercise 1 at the start of the chapter, his table of self-defeating thoughts and toxic beliefs – along with life-giving alternatives – might look like this:

Self-Defeating Thoughts and Beliefs	Life-Giving Thoughts and Beliefs
1. No one in the firm will care if I am bullied	1. While the people who run this firm appear not to care about the bullying that occurs in it, I do and I won't let myself be attacked
2. I am less important than a fee earner – I just work in the print media team	2. I don't earn fees for this firm – but I do a good job, deserve respect for doing it and deserve to be safe while I am at work
3. I can't stand up to aggressive people	3. I don't like aggression and I can say so
4. I'm technically minded, I'm not good with people	4. I have worked harder to learn technical skills than people skills – and I can address that imbalance
5. I'm submissive, it's in my nature, I just take abuse and don't fight back	5. I often use submissive behaviour at times when I need to be more assertive – I can learn some assertiveness skills so I can defend myself when I need to
6. Fighting back is pointless – it makes it worse	6. I can learn how to skilfully protect myself at the time of an attack

If the helpdesk technician is to defend himself effectively at the time of an attack, he needs to realise that his current thoughts are both negative and untrue. These two factors will then set him up for using self-protective behaviour when he needs to.

We have been exploring how self-defeating thinking and toxic beliefs can undermine your ability to act in your own best interests at the time of an attack. There is one more important issue we need to address in this chapter: what you might *feel* as a result of being subject to bullying behaviour.

Feeling Abandoned, Waiting for Rescue

An experience of workplace bullying can leave you feeling alone, anxious and afraid. The isolation can be most acute when one or more of your colleagues know that you are being bullied, either from witnessing incidents or from having heard about them afterwards, but apparently do nothing to support you. To be attacked in front of other people, be they colleagues, co-workers or customers, and discover that no one actively stands by you – no one says anything to defend you, to confront the bully or to comfort you after an attack – can be devastating. To learn that those who work alongside you know what is happening to you but don't subsequently support you, can leave you feeling dreadfully alone.

Some of my more traumatised clients were angrier at their senior managers for not confronting the bully than they were with the bully themselves. Feeling abandoned by managers, who are well aware of what is going on, can be a deeply disturbing experience as it calls the manager's integrity into question. Senior managers who recognise that there is bullying behaviour in their organisation, and don't confront it, actually *enable* it.

In addition to feeling abandoned, many people subject to bullying behaviour want to be rescued from the situation they find themselves in. Let's make a distinction between:

- A co-worker or manager who sees your distress, approaches you supportively, and talks with you about your experience of being bullied.

And:

- The desire that someone other than you – your manager, 'the organisation', even the bully themselves – magically alters your situation and rescues you from it.

The former can be vital and life-giving to someone who is being bullied. The latter is a way of thinking that doesn't serve you well. Strictly speaking, no one can rescue you. True Rescue is recognising the dynamics which you are currently creating in your life and choosing behaviour which creates different dynamics instead, dynamics which support your wellbeing and contribute towards your highest best interests. Waiting to be rescued is understandable, but it is not a wise use of your energy. Don't leave yourself in a vulnerable situation and merely wait for other people to intervene on your behalf. Intervene yourself. Learn the skills, tactics and tools you need to turn a losing situation into a winning one, so you turn the tables on the bully and regain your self-belief.

Summary of Key Points from the Chapter

Being subject to workplace bullying impacts how you behave, what you feel, what you think and what you believe. It results in shame, as you begin to think that it is somehow your fault that you are being targeted. Thinking it is your fault can result in you deciding that it is also your job to show the bully the error of their ways, and teach them how to handle their workplace relationships without recourse to bullying behaviour. And that simply isn't true and isn't a good use of your energy.

You need to confront the self-defeating thinking and toxic beliefs which create the illusion of your being powerless. Thinking you are powerless sets you up to use powerless behaviour, behaviour which leaves you vulnerable and encourages the bully. It sets up a self-fulfilling prophesy. Examples of powerless behaviour at the time of an attack include:

- Appealing to the bully's 'better nature'.

- Trying to reason with the bully.

- Trying to appease the bully.

- Feeling sorry for the bully.

- Using compliant behaviour and giving in to the bully's demands.

- Using avoidant behaviour and failing to confront the bully's aggression.

Complying and avoiding are not in your best interests. They play right into the bully's hands, allowing them to bully you without any resistance or consequences. It is much wiser to learn how to hold a bully accountable for their behaviour at the time of an attack, an approach which will enable you to retain control, power and self-esteem.

You may also feel abandoned, waiting to be rescued, but this way of thinking does not serve you well. You can learn self-protective and self-preserving behaviour and employ these skills at the time of an attack. Remember: the person bullying you is 100% responsible for their aggressive behaviour. That said, the most self-affirming thing you can do is learn to handle that behaviour effectively for yourself. The knowledge that you can retain control in the moment of an attack will do wonders for your self-esteem and confidence. It will give your spirits a huge lift to see yourself tackling bullying situations effectively, knowing that you are not vulnerable to attack in the way you once were, and recognising the new dynamics that your self-protective and self-preserving toolkit create for you.

The starting point in regaining your power, and being well prepared for any subsequent incidents of bullying behaviour, is to challenge your own toxic, self-defeating thinking and beliefs. The insidious thoughts and beliefs that imply you are powerless or helpless are not accurate. Challenge them and replace them with more accurate, truthful beliefs about yourself. Use the energy which is fuelling your toxic thinking to learn how to retain control at the time of an attack.

Questions for You to Consider

You may now like to identify a situation in which you were targeted at work. Bring a specific situation to mind and then answer the following questions about it. You can jot down your answers to each of the questions in the space below it:

1. What was the situation? What happened during it?

2. How did you respond at the time?

3. Looking back at your responses to exercise 1: to what extent did your self-defeating thinking and toxic beliefs affect your response at the time of the attack?

4. To what extent did you use avoidance and compliance as strategies to help you get through the attack?

5. Looking back on it now, what could you have said or done differently that might have been more self-protective and self-preserving for you?

Next Chapter

Chapter 4 focuses on grooming. It explores what grooming is, what it feels like and why it can be so confusing. The chapter highlights a range of well-intentioned but ineffective strategies for handling grooming, as well as a range of powerful responses to use at the time of an incident.

Chapter 4
How Bullies Groom

Why Grooming is Confusing, How to Resist It

What is Grooming?

This chapter explores grooming: the behaviour used by a bully to ascertain whether you, a potential target, will be susceptible to a campaign of workplace bullying. Grooming occurs during the period *before* the campaign against you commences. It may occur just once, or over a number of interactions. In each incident of grooming, the bully deliberately uses behaviour which tests the waters to see how you react. They then carefully observe what you say and do, and make an assessment about whether you will be someone with whom they will find it straightforward to create a bullying dynamic. This is grooming and every workplace bully does it.

Absolutely anyone can be groomed. People who are assertive and know how to handle confrontation can be groomed. People who don't like conflict or don't know how to stand up for themselves can be groomed. But not everyone will be subject to a *campaign* of workplace bullying. In many cases, people who have a hard time using assertive behaviour may be the preferred targets for workplace bullies because their responses at the time of being groomed leave them vulnerable. But it is also true to say that self-assured and confident people can be as bewildered and hurt as the more timid person should they be subject to a campaign of workplace bullying.

Some bullies move rapidly from grooming their potential targets to bullying them within a matter of seconds. Others take longer to make their assessment of who to target for a campaign. In this case, they make their decision following a number of grooming interactions, weighing up who responds more vulnerably and less vulnerably to their carefully chosen tactics. Some bullies observe how a potential target interacts with *other* people, and weigh up this information along with their personal experiences of the potential target.

Grooming can be subtle and confusing, or it can be direct and obvious. But, however the bully conducts their grooming encounters, they have one aim in mind: to assess how you react as they groom you. Specifically, they are likely to evaluate:

- How you receive their grooming behaviour: robustly, uncomfortably or somewhere in between.

- How effectively you protect your boundaries during the interaction.

- The degree to which you send back the message that you have understood what they are doing and know how to take care of yourself.

This chapter will examine a range of grooming behaviours that you may recognise from your experience at work. It will explore the intentions of workplace bullies as they groom you and identify a range of behaviours they might use as they do so. The chapter will discuss what it feels like to be groomed and why so many people who are groomed don't realise the significance of the confusing behaviour they are subject to. The case studies and examples in the chapter highlight the intentions of would-be bullies as they groom, and a range of effective and ineffective responses to grooming. The chapter concludes by highlighting how to respond effectively to an incident of grooming so that you send back a clear message to the would-be bully that you will not be a straightforward target for them.

> **Grooming is a set of behaviours bullies use to test out which potential targets will be most susceptible to a campaign of bullying.**

Early Warning Signs

If you have experience of being bullied at work, you will recognise a moment when the *campaign* against you started. At that point the bully was aggressive towards you in an attempt to introduce a bullying dynamic into their relationship with you. They may have:

- Been abusive towards you out of the blue.

- Taken advantage of your fear and confusion to seize control of the interaction.

- Used your fear to keep you wrong-footed and self-doubting.

- Intimidated you in front of other people in the expectation that no one would intervene on your behalf and you would feel isolated.

There are many potential starting points for a workplace bully who has decided to move into a campaign against you. But why did the bully target you in the first place? Why did they single you out as opposed to someone else? What happened prior to the commencement of the campaign, which encouraged them to target you? Consider these three short examples:

- A friendly, warm nurse joins a new specialist team as part of her planned hospital rotation. The nurse is known for her ready ability to build rapport with her colleagues and is used to being liked for her generosity and openness. Most of her new colleagues are welcoming and set time aside to spend with her during her first week, either over lunch or coffee. She is excited by the opportunity to learn new skills on the rotation and by the apparent friendliness of most people in the team. However, things take a different turn on the Friday afternoon of her first week when she finds herself with one of the senior nurses in the kitchen. The senior nurse has been superficially polite and responsive to the new nurse during the week without being either warm or accessible. But, nonetheless, the new nurse is pleased with the way her first week has gone and is off guard and relaxed in the company of the more senior figure. They talk about this and that, and then the senior nurse turns towards her more junior colleague, stiffens her upper body, looks down her nose at her and says the words: 'You are an intimidating woman' in a cold, hard tone. The new nurse is completely thrown at being characterised as intimidating. She is used to being liked for her approachable and warm personality, and cannot account for how she could be perceived as intimidating. Her mind reels. She mentally replays her encounters with the senior nurse during that week trying to identify something she might have said or done which could have been construed as 'intimidating.' Her confusion renders her briefly speechless, and in the second or two it takes her to feel dismayed she can't find anything to say. The senior nurse takes the opportunity to turn smartly on her heels and walk briskly out of the kitchen, leaving her new colleague feeling unsettled and unaccountably disturbed. From that moment onwards, the senior nurse makes a point of bullying the newcomer every time she is alone with her, but never in public.

- A public relations consultancy is run by two long-term business partners who decide to recruit an experienced and successful freelancer to join their team. After a short search, the slightly older partner interviews one particular candidate, thinks highly of her, and decides then and there to recruit her. He tells his younger business partner that he has found the ideal person to join their group, and arranges to introduce the freelancer to the team. The freelancer had run her own business single-handedly for the previous three years, and plans to bring her contacts and clients with her. She is pleased that she will now be part of a team and have ready colleague support to call on in the weeks and months ahead. She had begun to find working alone quite tough, and is relieved that she can expect to talk over important project and client-handling issues with her new colleagues. She agrees to sign a contract of employment and arranges to meet all the existing team members on an individual basis, starting with the younger business partner. She is already in the meeting room at the consultancy's green field site when the younger partner opens the door and steps unsmilingly into the room. The freelancer is aware of his lack of warmth, but thinks nothing of it, so enthusiastic is she to meet her new colleague. As the younger partner takes a seat he says, 'I gather there was quite a meeting of minds between you and my business partner.' The freelancer is taken aback by this characterisation of her selection interview with the older partner. She thought they got on well enough and that there would be a good fit between her skill-set and the consultancy's existing portfolio, but she did not think that the two of them had formed a particularly close bond. She prepares to disagree with the younger business partner and set the record straight. But some instinct for self-preservation prevents her from opening her mouth and she does not verbalise the thought in her head. The moment passes and the meeting continues. In the days ahead this business partner undermines the new recruit in one-to-one meetings between them, characterising her work as 'boring' and 'dull', replying with one-line terse and critical responses to her requests for feedback on her proposals, and calling her clients behind her back to check that they are satisfied with the work she is doing for them. Over the next twelve months, he continues to bully the new colleague until the former freelancer decides that enough is enough. She resigns and returns, bruised and fatigued, to working alone as a freelance consultant.

- Two administrative assistants in a large pharmaceutical company fall out over lunch. One of them is unaccountably and severely rude to the other. Despite their having been friends as well as colleagues for a couple of years, the rude administrative assistant arranges a curry that evening with other people from the team, omitting to invite the second administrative assistant to it. During the meal, the rude administrative assistant is repeatedly asked why her friend and colleague is not present, and realises she has overstepped the mark. The following day, she seeks her out to apologise, telling her that she was rude to her and wrong to omit her from the meal she arranged. The wronged assistant is gracious and humble in response, telling her colleague that she is forgiven and they needn't refer to it again. She suggests they have lunch together that day. The following day the two of them are in their joint office clearing up mugs and plates following the mid-morning break. The assistant who apologised turns towards her colleague, folds her arms and tells her that some people are good at apologising. She maintains level eye contact with her colleague as she says these words. Her energy is edgy and uncomfortable. Her colleague doesn't understand what she is being told nor does she recognise the mood which has come over her colleague. Frightened to damage the renewed connection between them by mishandling the moment, and still cherishing the apparently sincere apology which she received the previous day, she decides not to say anything, lets the moment pass and leaves the room. During the remainder of that week, and during the month that follows, her 'friend' bullies her relentlessly in a subtle campaign of workplace bullying. She leaves her out of information-giving loops, fails to address points she puts to her in team meetings, and refuses to make eye contact with her when she enters a room or speaks to her informally. Her subtle bullying becomes blatant when, at the end of the month, she finally rounds on her friend in the kitchen. She angrily accuses her of deliberately undermining her relationships with the other people on the team, claims that she has been working to destroy her reputation behind her back, and storms out of the room. Her colleague is stunned and shaken. She certainly has not said anything untoward about her colleague to anyone on the team, has not undermined her reputation and has remained positive and constructive in her dealings with her despite being put under considerable pressure by her for over a month. In fact, it is the other way round. Her colleague *is* guilty of undermining *her* reputation and sullying *her* character, both of which she has been doing consistently as part of her campaign of workplace bullying.

Mishandling the Moment

In each of these shorter examples one colleague is subject to grooming by another, does not recognise the encounter for what it is - an attempt to prepare the ground for a campaign to follow – and becomes subject to workplace bullying. Let's re-visit the action in each case to see what we can learn about the nature of the grooming which occurred on each occasion. We will examine each example, firstly from the point of view of the colleague subject to grooming behaviour; secondly, from the point of view of the bully; and thirdly, to understand the nature of the interaction between them that rendered the first colleague vulnerable to a subsequent campaign of bullying. Let's start with the interaction between the new nurse and her more senior colleague.

- The new nurse is an open and sunny character, used to establishing rapport with her colleagues quite quickly. She likes people and recognises that she is usually liked in return for her warm and accessible way with people. On joining her new team, she is eager to fit in and keen to get on well with her new colleagues. She makes a good impression with most people, and finds that the majority of her colleagues are welcoming. She is off guard and relaxed when, at the end of her first week, she finds herself alone in the kitchen with one of the senior nurses on the team. The senior nurse is a brittle character: slightly aloof and without the easy way with people which the new nurse possesses. She has watched her young colleague's entry to the team with a suspicious eye, noted her popularity and her social ease. She is jealous and aloof towards her younger colleague, but plays her cards close to her chest. She gives no clue about her jealousy until the two of them are alone in the kitchen at the end of the new nurse's first week. Only then, when her colleague is relaxed and off guard, does the senior nurse reveal her true agenda. She subjects the new nurse to a carefully controlled incident of grooming in which she characterises her in terms which are untrue, hurtful and unexpected. The new nurse is anything but 'intimidating' and having been described in this way she is completely thrown. Her mind reels as she tries to account for what she might have said or done that could be construed as 'intimidating'. As her mind goes blank she cannot think of anything to say. *And in that moment the senior nurse learns that when she directs a well-judged personal insult at the new nurse it hits home and the new nurse does not know how to protect herself from the insult or to re-join the fight.* From that moment onwards the senior nurse repeats the tactic: she takes advantage of the fact that the new nurse isn't used to being disliked and needs to be thought well of by her seniors. She uses her seniority in the team as a weapon against the new nurse, to punish her and to attack her. But only in private, when the two of them are alone together, and never in public when she might be held to account for her unkind comments by another colleague.

Let's now turn to the second example which involved the freelance consultant who joins a small, established public relations firm. Once again, we will start our analysis from the perspective of the freelancer, before moving on to explore the motives of the bullying business partner, and finally examine the nature of the interaction between them which renders the freelancer vulnerable to being bullied.

The freelance consultant has found working alone hard going in recent months. She is pleased and relieved to be offered the chance to work with colleagues in a team environment, and looks forward to being able to talk through challenging and important work issues with supportive team mates. It is true that she made a very quick decision to join the consultancy jointly run by the business partner she meets at the selection interview. Indeed, she only spent two hours with this partner, and didn't meet any of the other people in the firm before she agreed to sign a contract of employment. We can say with some certainty that she allowed her relief at being offered a way out of her isolated freelance existence to cloud her judgement, because she doesn't really know enough about the group of people she is to join before she agrees to work with them. In particular, she hasn't even met the younger business partner who part-owns the firm. Having already made an emotional commitment to work with the team, the freelancer is unprepared for the way in which the younger business partner grooms her as soon as he meets her.

The younger business partner does not welcome the freelancer. He dislikes the possibility that the newcomer will upset the balance between him and his business partner. They have worked together for a long time, running the business in tandem, and while he accepts that they need another income generator he is ambivalent about the prospect of another energetic and potentially troublesome addition to the team. He doesn't want the, as he sees it, competition. He doesn't want to lose influence with the older business partner or have to jockey for position and power with the newcomer. Rather than face his fears, he sets about unsettling the newcomer and grooms her as soon as he meets her. What he says on entering the meeting room is both a challenge and a clear message about the nature of the threat he perceives the freelancer to represent to him and his place in his business.

He says: 'I gather there was quite a meeting of minds between you and my business partner.' This form of words is quite revealing. It conveys three distinct, but related things. Firstly, that the younger business partner sees his relationship with the older business partner in proprietorial terms. He says 'my business partner', not Mike which is the business partner's name. This reveals his possessive and insecure nature. Secondly, his words suggest that he and his business partner have had a conversation about the freelancer's selection interview at which he concluded that there had been a meeting of minds. Whether there had or had not been such a conversation – and, in fact, there hadn't been – is not the point. The younger business partner wishes to suggest to the freelancer that the nature of the bond between the two of them had been an open topic of discussion behind her back. This is quite deliberate and is designed to put doubt into the freelancer's mind in two ways: why should the older business partner suggest there had been a meeting of minds when there hadn't? What does such a discussion say about how she will be viewed by the other existing members of the workforce? Thirdly, the unsmiling and cold demeanour of the younger business partner sends a clear signal to the newcomer that she is not welcome. The freelancer is by no means unassertive. She runs her own successful business, and is confident and able interpersonally. She initially wants to disagree with the younger business partner but, sadly for her, she hesitates before changing her mind. Her hesitation is borne out of an instinct for self-preservation.

Her intuition correctly warns her that the person in the room could be dangerous. Unfortunately for her, when she makes the split second decision to remain silent, she makes the wrong decision. Letting the moment pass was not a wise way to handle this adversary. The younger business partner learns that he can drop mischievous and misleading material onto the table and the freelancer will ignore it. This is exactly the dynamic he wishes to assess, and it gives him the green light to proceed to a campaign of workplace bullying. Although the freelancer eventually decides that enough is enough and leaves the firm, she has become so confused and self-doubting, and is so reluctant to return to working alone, that it takes her a year to come to this decision. She is exhausted when she is finally able to take the self-preserving step she needs to take, and decides to work by herself again.

Now let's turn to the third example which features the two administrative assistants. We will start our analysis from the perspective of the wronged assistant, move on to explore the motives of the bullying assistant, and then examine the nature of the interaction between them which renders the wronged assistant vulnerable to being bullied. This is a particularly shocking example of grooming and bullying in the workplace because it involves one friend and colleague turning on another.

- The wronged administrative assistant is a sincere if naïve character. She is also a loyal and forgiving friend. She cherishes the apology which is apparently sincerely offered to her by her friend and colleague, and quickly puts behind her both her colleague's rudeness and her deliberate failure to include her in the curry evening. She quite genuinely moves on from these two unfortunate incidents and thinks no more about them, so glad is she that the two of them are friends again and can companionably share an office. They have lunch together and, as far as the wronged assistant is concerned, that is that. It doesn't occur to her that the episode isn't done with as far as her colleague is concerned and is, in fact, the tip of an iceberg. The following day she finds herself clearing up with her friend in their shared office following mid-morning coffee. She does not recognise the other assistant's edgy and tense mood, nor does she know how to interpret her strange words when she says: 'Some people are good at apologising.' She is flummoxed by these words, and the weird energy with which her friend and colleague articulates them. She is caught between two stools. She could simply say 'what do you mean?' or 'what are you talking about?' But somehow she can't manage to say either because she is confused. Only the day before her colleague had apologised to her, apparently quite sincerely, so the implication that some apologies are hard to give doesn't make sense to her. The wronged administrative assistant does not want to go back over old ground and wants to believe that the apology she received was genuinely meant. She does not want to entertain the thought that it wasn't an authentic apology, but was a ruse designed to put her off guard and set her up, something which is unthinkable to such an honest and good-natured woman. Her colleague watches her discomfort with interest. The rude assistant is a duplicitous and complicated character. She is not remorseful about leaving her friend out of the curry evening.

She makes her apology because she feels cornered. She is taken by surprise when the other members of the team want to know where the wronged assistant is and why she isn't at the meal. They won't let the subject drop. Peer pressure – not integrity - causes the rude assistant to apologise the following day. But the fact that she has apologised rankles with her, and she looks for an opportunity to turn the tables on her friend again. When the two of them are alone in their joint office, she reveals her true nature. She becomes edgy and awkward as she prepares to groom her friend. She makes a remark that doesn't, on the face of it, make much sense and watches her colleague to see how she reacts. She notices the confusion on her friend's face, observes that she mentally decides not to ask her what she means, and is satisfied when she leaves the room confused and without challenging her back. The scene is set for her to move into a campaign of bullying someone whose personal qualities and genuine integrity she envies. Over the course of the next month she attacks her to her face both subtly and at every opportunity, and injures her reputation behind her back whenever she can. Her final outrageous attack is calculated and nasty. She accuses her, in raging tones, of undermining *her* reputation: the very thing she herself is guilty of. This groundless attack is borne out of a combination of her shame and guilt. After all, she *is* guilty of these very actions. But in accusing the person she has wronged for the past month, she displays a pernicious and vicious capacity to injure and confuse her colleague simply because she can.

What Bullies Look for When they Groom

In each of these examples, one colleague is successfully groomed by another because of a combination of factors. In each case, the person subject to grooming mishandles the moment because they:

- Don't recognise the grooming behaviour for what it is.

- Feel confused about what just happened.

- Feel intimidated and can't say what they would normally say in response to the confusing behaviour or ask the obvious question.

- Don't want to face up to the challenging dynamics they find themselves in, so keep quiet when they really need to speak up.

- Feel vulnerable because they want to make a good impression, have invested emotionally in a job or friendship, want to be liked or want to make a contribution which will be valued by an authority figure.

- Feel uncertain or self-doubting and avoid the confrontation they need to have.

Workplace bullies thrive on these factors. They are on the look-out for them. They observe how their grooming is received by a potential target and, once they have recognised the confusion and vulnerability they are looking for, it is easy for them to move into a campaign. Many bullies possess highly-sensitive radars for these dynamics. They somehow pick up on vulnerability and confusion, and having recognised them in a potential target, quickly seek to exploit the opportunity to introduce a bullying dynamic into their relationship with that person.

Bullies are on the look-out for evidence of confusion or vulnerability in those they groom.

But, in each of the above examples there *was* an opportunity for the colleague subject to grooming to retain their power and respond effectively at the time of being groomed. Had each of them known what to say to prevent the bullying dynamic from being established, things would have turned out quite differently for them. We will return to each of these examples at the end of the chapter to identify what each of them could have said or done differently that would have been self-protective and gone some way to preventing their would-be assailant from moving into a campaign of bullying. But first, let's explore one more example of grooming.

Each of the examples above involves one colleague grooming another while the two of them are alone. What about a more complicated case study where the would-be bully grooms a colleague in full view of everyone in the department?

Case Study 3: Groomed

An editorial assistant who has been without work for two months is offered a job on a fashion magazine. Delighted and relieved to be employed again after being made redundant from his previous employer, the editorial assistant starts work in a busy department of twenty people. The entire team is located in the same open plan office, each person having a screened off desk, with the head of department in an office in one corner. The atmosphere in the office is industrious, if a little formal for his tastes, but the editorial assistant finds the people sitting near him friendly and open on his first day. The head of department, whom he had met at interview, makes a point of coming to his desk in the morning and the afternoon of his first day. He is flattered that she would bother to come and speak with him, and stands up as she approaches his desk. However, he finds both encounters with her a little stilted and uncomfortable. She uses a patronising tone and speaks down to him, as if he is a child she wishes to belittle. On the first occasion, he responds politely and efficiently to her questions about whether he knows where the toilets are, and whether he had been shown where the tea and coffee making facilities are. On the second occasion, he finds her manner just as awkward to deal with as she tells him briskly that there is a lot for him to be getting on with. On neither occasion does she ask him about the work he has been assigned, how he is settling into the office or about his reactions to his first day at work. On both occasions, despite being pleased that she bothered to single him out for attention, he is relieved when she leaves to return to her office. He notices that none of the team members sitting near his desk look up as she approaches or say hello to her. Everyone continues with their work, heads down, apparently deep in concentration.

Over the next two weeks, every time the head of department walks past his desk or meets him in a corridor she takes the opportunity to bully him. She might stop at his desk, ostensibly to find out how he is getting on, and refer to the work he is doing as 'his playtime'. She might touch him lightly on the shoulder as she walks past his desk and, without breaking step, comment: 'you do the work and I'll tell you where you've gone wrong.' Or, using an openly derogatory tone, she might ask one of the people sitting near him: 'How's the newbie settling in?' It is the hidden sub-text to these remarks that is so unsettling for the editorial assistant. On the lips of another more open, sunny and personable manager, each of them could be taken as a warm-hearted, friendly comment. But, on the lips of the head of department, they take on a different and less innocent character. Each time she makes one of these remarks, the editorial assistant freezes as he tries to weigh up if he is imagining things and becoming paranoid, or whether she is, as he fears, putting him down.

Every time she makes a belittling comment, speaks down to him, is openly patronising or makes an unpleasant remark, the head of department immediately laughs it off as 'a bit of banter between them.' In team meetings, she peppers her verbal exchanges with him with unpleasant comments, but also makes a point of using just enough reasonable and encouraging behaviour that he thinks it might be him who needs to toughen up and not take things so personally. At the end of his second week of employment following a lengthy team meeting, she corners him in the coffee room and tells him that no one else in the department likes him. The editorial assistant is shocked and flounders. He has not picked up any dislike from his colleagues. Indeed, he thinks he is getting on quite well with the people who sit near him. As he tries to formulate a response to this attack, the head of department turns on her heels and, as she walks away from him, tells him over her shoulder that she has some ideas for improving his work on his current assignment. The editorial assistant is dismayed that the standard of his work is being criticised after just hearing that he is not well liked in the department.

He arranges a meeting with the head of department in her office that afternoon. He has very mixed feelings about arranging this meeting. The head of department didn't specifically ask him to arrange a meeting, but he feels that he ought to meet her if he is to hear her suggestions for improving the quality of his work. He is apprehensive about what she might say. At the meeting, the head of department makes a number of suggestions for changing the way he approaches his assignment, all of which are fine, but none of which improves its quality. The editorial assistant feels his judgement is being undermined.

He goes back to his desk, shoulders drooping, and sits glumly staring at his computer screen. The colleague at the nearest desk to his swivels her chair towards him and asks him what's wrong. He quietly tells her that he is finding it hard to deal with the head of department, to which she responds, 'well, she's like that with everyone' and turns back to her work. The editorial assistant is not at all sure that she is like that with everyone. He hasn't heard her patronise anyone else in the team as blatantly as she patronises him, and feels increasingly sure that she reserves her most castigating behaviour for him. He starts to feel vulnerable and unsure. He doesn't feel he can say anything to her directly: she is the head of department. He doesn't think any of his colleagues are interested in discussing the issues with him, and certainly none of them support him at the time of an attack even though they are present when many of them occur. He feels trapped and doesn't quite know what to do. He tells himself that he is inexperienced, she is the head of department, she knows her job and how to manage the team, and he should be less sensitive. That night he tells his girlfriend that his head of department seems to be bullying him. She listens, reflects for a moment, and replies that he ought to be careful how he handles her because he might be provoking her in some way.

Analysing the Dynamics in Case Study 3: Groomed

Let's examine the dynamics at play in this case study in which a newly-recruited editorial assistant is groomed by his head of department on his first day, and is then subject to a campaign of workplace bullying. We will discuss the ways in which the well-intentioned but ineffective response of the editorial assistant to being groomed encourages the head of department, and the way in which the team's silent endorsement of her behaviour adds to the challenges facing him. Then we will identify what he could have said and done differently at the moment of being groomed, to send back a message to his new manager that should she decide to target him he will be well placed to defend himself appropriately. Let's start by looking inside his life for insight into why he mishandles the two grooming incidents.

The editorial assistant needs a job. He has been unemployed for two months and needs to start earning again. In the competitive world of magazine publishing, two months is a long time to be without employment and he is relieved and delighted to be offered a role with the magazine. He had met his new head of department at the selection interview, but it is only when he joins her department and is, as she sees it, within her control that she starts to groom him.

On his first day she approaches him at his desk twice, once in the morning and again in the afternoon. On seeing him approach, the respectful new employee gets to his feet in deference to his new manager. He assumes that she has come to welcome him and is grateful for her interest. She notes his politeness and is pleased by what it tells her about him. During the two grooming interactions that day the head of department is by turns patronising, belittling and demeaning towards her new team member, both in the tone she uses while speaking with him and in the subject matter she chooses to discuss with him. She asks him if he knows where the toilet is and if he knows where the coffee and tea facilities are. These questions are calculating: they are not genuine enquiries. They are designed to put him on the back foot so she can see how he reacts. His reaction is what she hoped for: slightly nonplussed and a bit bemused. She decides that the way is clear for her to move into a campaign of bullying.

Let's now take a look at the way in which the silent complicity of the rest of the team add to the challenge facing the editorial assistant as he tries to come to terms with the head of department's behaviour towards him. The head of department conducts both of the grooming interactions on his first day in full view of everyone else in the team. She approaches him at his desk in an open plan office, confident that no one in the room will challenge her as she softens up the new recruit. How does she know this? Because she is a practised bully who has created a culture of subtle and more blatant bullying in the department over a considerable period of time, and she knows full well that everyone in the team is aware of her tactics and lets her get away with it. Some people have left the department, but all those currently employed in it either turn a blind eye to her grooming and bullying, accept that that is the price to be paid for having a job with the magazine, or actively collude with her by feeding information and gossip about selected colleagues. The misguided team members who do this have adopted the view that to be her ally is better than to be her enemy. They are quite wrong. Their habit of colluding with her by feeding her information and gossip will not prevent her from targeting them should she be minded to.

The colleagues sitting nearest to the editorial assistant all hear the content and tone of the two grooming conversations which occur on his first day at work. They are well aware what their manager is up to. None of them warns the new recruit. None of them gives him so much as a sympathetic glance after she leaves his desk. The fact that no one seems to notice how patronising and rude she is confuses the editorial assistant. Instead of seeing it for the red flag it is – clear evidence of a bullying culture in the department – he thinks he might have been overly sensitive and gets on with his work. In fact, he isn't being overly sensitive at all. He is spot on. His boss is a dangerous person to work for, someone who wants to injure his self-esteem and undermine his confidence. Two weeks later, when the campaign of bullying against him is well established, the editorial assistant does mention his confusion to one of the people sitting near him. Her response - that the head of department is always like that - isn't at all reassuring. In fact, it is another red flag that the editorial assistant needs to take note of. He needs to fully take on board that the people who sit around him know exactly what is happening to him, misrepresent it as usual behaviour throughout the department, and downplay its significance. In doing so, they all passively collude with the head of department in an attempt to avoid being targeted next.

So, what could the new recruit have said or done differently at the time of being groomed which would have sent back a clear message to the head of department that he may be new but he also knows how to take care of himself? The new recruit could have simply played back her patronising words to the head of department in the form of a question. When she asks him out of the blue if he knows where the toilet is, he needs to politely but firmly say, 'where the toilet is?' with a slight emphasis on the word 'toilet' and with his voice rising at the end of the phrase to denote it is a question. Using this form of words achieves three things for him. Firstly, it holds up a mirror to the head of department so that she can see how she appears when she asks that question. It changes the point of the conversation so that the momentum and control is now with the editorial assistant. Secondly, it requires the head of department to find a response to her own question, something she will not be expecting and which will momentarily throw her. Thirdly, the editorial assistant no longer needs to find an answer to her impertinent question.

Had he been able to say this to her, he would have succeeded in thwarting her attempt to create a bullying dynamic with him that time round. He would have preserved his personal power and drawn a clear boundary around her intrusive comment. He would have sent her the message that she can continue to belittle him if she wants, but he and he alone decides what he feels, where the boundary between them lies, and how far he will let her encroach. Crucially, it would have told her that he owns his personal power fully, and while he accepts and respects that she is his boss, he reserves the right to decide for himself where the line between them will be placed.

While handling this pivotal moment well wouldn't necessarily prevent her from trying to groom him again – only she can make that decision - it will give her considerable pause for thought.

> **Colleagues who turn a blind eye to incidents of bullying are colluding with a bullying culture.**

Handling Grooming Effectively

Let's now return to the three examples from earlier in the chapter so that we can identify what each of the main characters subject to grooming could have said or done differently. In each case, we will identify simple but powerful strategies that they could have used to protect themselves, strategies which preserve their power and make it less likely that the would-be bully would easily be able to create a bullying dynamic with them.

- When the senior nurse turns towards her in the kitchen and says: 'you are an intimidating woman' the friendly nurse needs to stay in the conversation. She mustn't go silent and let the moment pass, even if she feels shocked and confused. She needs to use a light but clear tone to say to the more senior person, 'I don't see myself like that'. This response tells the senior nurse that her self-image is her own concern, and she is the final judge of who she is. It tells the senior nurse that she may well find her junior colleague intimidating, but that even if she does, the new nurse is not dismayed at being characterised like that. This clever response puts the issues back to the senior nurse, and challenges what the senior nurse is trying to do: take her junior colleague's power away by playing on her need to be liked, characterising her in a way which is the opposite of how she – and most other people – see her.

- When the younger business partner enters the room and says 'I gather there was quite a meeting of minds between you and my business partner' the freelancer needs to challenge him straight back. In a straightforward relaxed tone she needs to say either 'why do you say that?' or say 'I don't agree. I thought there was a good skill fit between me and the firm, but no particular meeting of minds with your business partner.' These two responses achieve slightly different things. The question requires the younger business partner to justify what he has just said, something he will find quite difficult to do because it isn't true. The statement about what the freelancer actually thinks tells the younger business partner that the freelancer knows her own mind, isn't afraid of confrontation and is quite able to disagree when she needs to. Either way of handling the moment will change the momentum of the conversation, taking it away from the younger business partner and redressing the power imbalance he is trying to create between them.

- When her friend and colleague turns towards her and tells her that some people are good at apologising, the gullible but good-natured administrative assistant needs to find out what she means. She needs to say: 'I don't understand what you just said. What does it mean?' This response requires that her colleague be transparent in what she is saying, stop playing a game where she is indirect and evasive, and put her cards on the table. It tells the dangerous administrative assistant that when she is indirect, devious and undermining, her good-natured colleague will not be flummoxed into silence and let the moment pass. The wronged assistant then needs to listen carefully to how her dangerous friend responds to her challenge before forming a view about how much she wishes to invest in this particular friendship from that point onwards.

> **Say: 'I don't see myself like that' to challenge an untrue, hurtful and undermining perception of you.**

> **When you are being groomed it's better to disagree and risk an argument rather than remain silent and risk being bullied.**

> **Say: 'What does that mean?' or 'I don't know what you just said' to get the issues into the open.**

Putting the Issue Back to the Bully

None of these effective ways of handling the incidents of grooming will necessarily prevent a campaign of bullying. But, by handling the grooming incidents in these effective ways, the colleague subject to grooming sends back a message to their would-be assailant that they know how to take care of themselves, are not easily going to give their power away, and won't be a straightforward person to target. By finding something to say which puts the issues back to the would-be bully, the person subject to grooming behaviour avoids the pitfall of letting the moment pass in avoidance and compliance thereby *giving their power away.*

In each of the examples we have been considering, the stakes are quite high for the colleague subject to grooming behaviour. Each of them may well feel that to challenge the would-be bully at the time of being groomed is a risky thing to do. But, in my view, not doing so represents a greater risk. To avoid the moment, and fail to push back, lets the would-be bully know that you will not fight back, don't know how to, and may be too frightened to: a combination of factors which will encourage them to target you.

However, even had each of the characters above been able to give these powerful responses at the time of being groomed, each of them would still need to be on the alert for subsequent occasions when their would-be bully might try and groom them again. On each subsequent occasion, they need to employ the same calm, unruffled, clear tone and put the issue back to the bully until they desist.

Summary of Key Points from the Chapter

Grooming is a set of behaviours used by workplace bullies to test out how susceptible you might be to a campaign of workplace bullying. Bullies choose to target people who have a hard time holding on to their personal power and with whom it will be more straightforward to create a bullying dynamic.

Grooming can be subtle and indirect, or blatant. If you are groomed it is vital that you realise what is happening and avoid remaining silent and passive. You need to find something to say, something which you articulate in a clear and relaxed tone. The very fact that you retain your composure sufficiently to reply to the grooming behaviour will tell the would-be bully that you know how to handle yourself. What you say, as well as how you say it, is quite important too. You could:

- Ask the bully what they mean if they are being indirect and evasive.

- Directly disagree with them to demonstrate that you know your own mind and are unafraid to say so.

- Challenge their perception of you by clarifying how you see yourself.

The very fact that you are confused at the moment of being groomed is the signal that you need to act. Don't hesitate. Say something back right at the moment of being perplexed. Your instinct that something is wrong is spot on. There is something untoward going on, so don't let the moment pass without making it clear that you see quite clearly what the would-be bully is trying to achieve.

Even when you have successfully defended yourself from grooming behaviour don't relax too much. Be aware that the would-be bully may try again, just to test your resolve and see how resilient you are. If they try again, then use exactly the same approach: put the issues back to them without being rude or disrespectful. Simply draw the line and keep doing it until they get the message and stop grooming you.

Questions for You to Consider

You may now like to identify a situation in which you were subject to grooming behaviour at work. Bring a specific situation to mind and then answer the following questions about it. You can jot down your answers to each of the questions in the space below it:

1. What was the situation? What happened during it?

2. What factors lead you to think you were groomed?

3. How did you respond at the time?

4. What impact did that response have on your subsequent interactions with the would-be bully?

5. Looking back on it now, what could you have said or done differently that would have sent back a clear message to your assailant that you know how to prevent them creating a bullying dynamic with you?

Next Chapter

Chapter 5 focuses in more detail on how to put the issues back to the bully at the time of an attack.

Chapter 5
Putting the Issues Back to the Bully

Using Different Behaviour to Create a Different Outcome

Preventing Emotional Overwhelm

For many of you, being subject to bullying means that you experience distress and emotional overwhelm. It means that you feel hurt, confused and disoriented after the attack for a period of hours, days or weeks. Your emotional overwhelm results in your energy levels dropping and your anxiety levels increasing as you anticipate another encounter with the bully.

But the good news is that it does not have to be like that. Putting the issues back to the bully effectively at the time of the attack means that you won't have to carry the backlog of distress and emotional overwhelm which are inevitable if the bully's assault on you succeeds. It means that the incident ends there, is done and dusted, and you can mitigate or entirely prevent emotional overwhelm.

There will be no emotional consequences for you to process afterwards because you have:

- Successfully altered the momentum of the interaction.

- Prevented the interaction focusing on you and your supposed 'faults.'

- Created consequences in the moment for the bully to deal with.

- Retained control.

- Preserved your personal power.

- Put your agenda on the table for the bully to respond to.

- Moved on emotionally as soon as the interaction is completed.

All of these positive outcomes are achievable, even for those of you who don't quite believe it.

In this chapter we will examine how to use behaviour in the moment of an attack which puts the issues back to the bully. We will explore how to exercise your choices wisely to alter the dynamic between you and the bully, re-arranging it so that it is more in your favour. We will examine a range of proven strategies and tactics which you may employ to achieve these goals, tools which will enable you to regain control of the interaction, leave the bully with plenty to think about and do so without resorting to aggressive or abusive behaviour. Let's make a start straight away.

> **You can prevent emotional overwhelm by putting the issues back to the bully at the time of the attack.**

Use a Different Behaviour, Create a Different Outcome

In Chapter 2, we explored how to confront your self-defeating thoughts and toxic beliefs and replace them with more truthful thoughts and beliefs. We noted how doing this alters the way you feel about yourself and sets you up to use positive, self-protective behaviour at the time of an attack. Let's take this principle one step further as we consider how *changing the way you behave* at the time of an attack – whether or not you have successfully addressed your self-defeating thoughts and toxic beliefs – will enable you to create a different and better outcome from that incident.

Consider the following diagram. It describes the relationship between a target's beliefs and fears, and the behaviour she uses when attacked. It then further illustrates how these behaviours influence the outcome of the attack. In this example, the target does a good job and has a supportive manager. The bully attacks her in her own office when she is alone. He is more senior in the organisation than she is and has a positive reputation. He employs the bullying methods of:

- Choosing his moment carefully, entering her office without knocking on the closed door and without an appointment.

- Shutting the door behind him as soon as he has entered the room.

- Standing in front of her desk with his legs apart, feet firmly planted on the floor and fists clenched.

- Launching into the attack as soon as he is in position.

- Aggressively criticising her work and character.

- Exaggerating small errors or stylistic anomalies in her work and portraying them as serious flaws.

- Using a demeaning, snide and cutting tone

The target's beliefs and fears	The target's behaviour at the time of an attack	Outcome of the attack
I am alone when he attacks me - he's senior and popular, no one will believe me	I remain quiet when the bully enters my office	
I am not good at standing up for myself - I don't know how to	I remain seated when he approaches my desk	The bully attacks my work standards, attitude and character
I don't like aggression and don't want to deal with aggressive people	I don't speak to him at all - I try to get the interaction over with quickly	I feel intimidated by his aggression and crushed by his words
I think his bullying will escalate if I fight back	I remain physically still throughout, trying not to let him know he has upset me	He leaves without me saying or doing anything to stop him bullying me
	I let the bully say and do what he wants so that he will leave quicker	He knows he can come back and bully me easily whenever he wants to

Diagram 2: The relationship between the target's beliefs and fears, her behaviour at the time of an attack, and the outcome of that attack

Changing the Game: Creating Consequences for the Bully

In this example, the target employs the strategy of remaining passive and silent in an attempt to get the abusive encounter over with as soon as possible. This well-intentioned approach leaves her wide open to being attacked whenever the bully is minded to attack her, because she is unable to say or do anything which prevents him from bullying her. Her compliant and avoidant demeanour make it hard for her to create just consequences for the bully to deal with or to alter the outcome of the attack in her favour. What would happen if she could handle the attack in such a way as to achieve both of these aims?

Consider the following amended diagram. You will note that her beliefs and fears are the same, *but her behaviour has changed, and her changed behaviour influences the outcome of the interaction in her favour.*

Your beliefs and fears	Your behaviour at the time of an attack	Outcome of the attack
I am alone when he attacks me - he's senior and popular, no one will believe me	I stand up behind my desk when the bully enters my office	The bully is less sure of himself
I am not good at standing up for myself - I don't know how to	I fold my arms when he approaches my desk	He blusters, saying he is too busy to write down his criticisms, and leaves saying 'do better or else'
I don't like aggression and don't want to deal with aggressive people	I ask him what he means when he says my work isn't up to scratch	I email my manager telling her that my work has been critiqued & I don't agree with the critique, that the manager involved declined to write his criticisms down, that I want a meeting with the 3 of us to discuss. I cc the bullying manager.
I think his bullying will escalate if I fight back	I tell him I want written feedback detailing his view of where my work is sub-standard so I can discuss it with my manager	

Diagram 3: How altering her behaviour at the time of the attack enables the target to alter the outcome of that attack in her favour

In this example the target successfully alters the dynamic between her and the bully by using different behaviour at the time of the attack. She goes onto the front foot and puts the issues back to him. Rather than remain passive and silent, she:

- *Stands up when he enters her office.* This active response tells him that he is entering her territory, and that she is in charge of that arena. It takes him by surprise because he is expecting her to be compliant and passive. This action starts the process of tipping the balance between them, altering it in her favour at the start of the interaction.

- *Folds her arms when he approaches her desk.* This self-protective stance sends him a clear message that she knows what is about to happen and is ready to defend herself. He is thrown but he quickly recovers and launches into his attack.

- *Puts a question to the bully.* She knows that her work is of a good enough standard, so she asks him what he means when he says her work isn't up to scratch. Her question halts him in his tracks, and requires the bully to justify his criticisms. This is not at all easy for him to do as his criticisms are fabrications and exaggerations designed to give him an excuse to bully her.

- *Tells him to write down his criticisms so she can discuss them with her manager.* She requires him to commit his critique to paper, and this stymies him. He isn't prepared to do so, as he has nothing factual to reproach her with. He blusters, says he is too busy and issues a final hollow threat. He says 'do better or else' as he leaves her office, on the back foot and trying to salvage some pride.

- *Emails her manager to inform her of what has happened, copying the bully into the email.* She breaks the cycle of silence surrounding the encounters between her and the bully by telling her manager that her work has been unjustly critiqued. She does not say 'I have been bullied.' She does not need to. She relays the facts: that her work has been criticised, that she has asked for written detail, that the manager concerned declines to provide it, and that she wants to meet with him and her manager to resolve the issues. She knows that her manager is supportive and will handle the meeting objectively. The bully must now attend the meeting and explain away what he has said or back down and decline the meeting. Neither will be an easy path for him to take. Either way, his bluff has been called and it is much less likely that he will enter the target's room unannounced in future with the aim of bullying her. She will need to be vigilant every time she has an encounter with him. He is a devious and potentially committed foe. But, by handling the attack so effectively she has turned the tables on him, and made it much more likely that he will think very hard indeed before attempting to bully her again. *His behaviour towards her will change* as he learns that she is quite able to defend herself, and quite able to create consequences for him to deal with should he choose to bully her.

Having handled things so well this time, *the target will now be well placed to go back and re-assess the beliefs and fears* which, up to that point, had kept her mired in submissive and self-defeating behaviour. Now that she has direct personal experience of successfully standing up to the bully, she can go back and confront her self-defeating beliefs and fears and replace them with truthful, life-giving thoughts and beliefs. Consider the following possibilities:

Self-Defeating Thoughts and Beliefs	Life-Giving Thoughts and Beliefs
1. I am alone when he attacks me - he's senior and popular, no one will believe me	1. I am by myself when he attacks me – and I can handle him perfectly well. I don't need anyone else to know about his bullying behaviour although I'd prefer it if they did. I can consider letting selected people know what he is doing
2. I am not good at standing up for myself - I don't know how to	2. I know exactly what to say and do to handle this bully effectively
3. I don't like aggression and don't want to deal with aggressive people	3. I hate aggression – but I can combat it perfectly well when I need to
4. I think his bullying will escalate if I fight back	4. The bullying didn't escalate when I put the issues back to the bully – in fact he didn't expect it, was thrown by it and left the room quickly

Key Issues: Responsibility and Truth

In this example the target is highly aware that her assailant has a positive reputation in the organisation, is more senior than her, and is popular. She does not think it will go well for her if she claims that he is bullying her, so instead she calls his bluff and asks him to justify his criticisms of her work. She does this because she knows that his criticisms are unjustified and that he cannot defend them. She asks him to write them down – to commit them to paper – so she can discuss them with her manager. She does this to call his bluff, fully expecting that he will not want to do so and that his bullying of her will abate or cease entirely. Her active, engaged and effective handling of the attack contributes to a positive outcome for her, and she is able to re-assess her thoughts and beliefs about herself.

Many of my clients are uncomfortable at the prospect of putting the issues back to the bully when I first start to work with them. Like the target in the above example, some clients don't know how to put the issues back safely and become worried that they will do so without sufficient skill and make the situation worse. Others are afraid of reprisals. They worry that, if they confront the bully, the attacks will escalate. Other clients have philosophical challenges to overcome, challenges that you may be experiencing too. Let's take a look at two of them.

You may not want to put the issues back to the bully because:

- You think that doing so will mean you are attacking them back, and you don't want to counter-attack because it will mean that you behave like them.

- You think that to do so will be like seeking revenge, and you don't want to act like that.

Putting the issues back to the bully is not about attacking them back. Nor is it about revenge. It is about responsibility and truth. It is about putting the responsibility for what the bully is saying and doing where it rightly belongs: with the bully. It is about requiring them to take responsibility for what they are doing and cease doing it. It is about making a clear distinction between what they say – a mixture of slander, exaggeration, lies, aggressive insults and destructive intentions – and what is actually true. It is about making the fact of the matter – they are bullying you – the central point, not the noise and fog the bully creates about you or your performance.

The good news is that it is my experience that truth always trumps bullying noise, and that holding a bully responsible for what they are saying at the time they are saying it always interrupts their flow, and sometimes completely defeats them.

> **Using a different behaviour at the time of an attack will create a different outcome.**

> **Putting the issues back to the bully is about truth and responsibility – not revenge or counter-attack.**

Exercise 2: Your Behaviour at the Time of an Attack

You may now like to create your own diagram to clarify how your beliefs and fears influence the behaviour you use at the time of the attack, and how that behaviour influences the outcome of the attack.

Call to mind a specific incident in which you were bullied. Complete the middle box first, describing what you did at the time of the attack. Then complete the third box, describing the outcomes you experienced at the time. Lastly, complete the first box, capturing the self-defeating beliefs and fears which influenced your behaviour. You may like to refer back to Exercise 1: Tackling Self-Defeating Thoughts and Toxic Beliefs in Chapter 3 as you complete this last box.

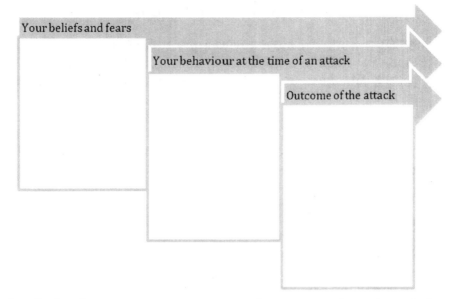

Your beliefs and fears

Your behaviour at the time of an attack

Outcome of the attack

I will shortly encourage you to complete a second version of the diagram so that you can plan to use different behaviour in a similar situation. To provide you with food for thought about what you might do differently, I'd like to re-visit Case Study 2 from Chapter 3 to see what lessons we can take from it.

Returning to Case Study 2 : Paralysed : How to Regain Control at the Time of the Attack

When we left the action, a helpdesk technician had been bullied on the telephone and then again face-to-face by an abusive, raging fee earner. During both attacks he remained passive and compliant. Let's return to the case study to identify:

- What the helpdesk technician might have done differently at the time of the telephone attack to put the issues back to the abusive fee earner.

- What measures he could have taken after the first attack to protect himself and his team colleagues from the second attack.

- What measures he could have taken during the second face-to-face attack to put the issues back to the bully.

- What the other members of the print media team could have done to stand alongside their colleague during the second attack, and create effective consequences for the bully to deal with.

Let's start with what the helpdesk technician could have done differently at the time of the first telephone attack to put the issues back to the abusive fee earner. His options are limited, but he does have some.

When he picks up the telephone and is immediately subject to a verbal assault, the helpdesk technician needs to see the moment for what it is: an unwarranted and raging attack by a colleague in his workplace. He needs to act straightaway. He must not remain passive and submissive as this demeanour will work against him. It will be difficult for him to speak over the caller and demand that he stop shouting at him and speak in a normal voice. The fee earner does not draw breath during his verbal assault. So, as soon as he hears the raging tone and abusive words of the fee earner, the helpdesk technician needs to consider replacing the receiver. Ending the call by replacing the receiver draws a very clear boundary between him and his assailant. It won't necessarily stop the fee earner from coming to his office to confront him. But, it will give the fee earner the clear message that he won't be intimidated into submission and can say no. Unfortunately for him, the helpdesk technician does not do this. He allows the fee earner the space and room during the call to say anything he wants for as long as he wants.

Let's now consider the crucial period of time between the two attacks. What measures could the helpdesk technician have taken after the telephone assault and before the face-to-face encounter to protect himself and his team colleagues?

The five minute period between the two attacks is vital. During that period of time, the helpdesk technician needs to confront the fact that he has just been bullied on the telephone. This is the case even if he succeeds in replacing the receiver during the call. He needs to take seriously the threat that the bully may come down to his office to find out where the report covers are, and that during that visit he may once again indulge his desire to rage. The helpdesk technician needs to warn his colleagues that a furious senior figure may be about to descend on them. He needs to tell them to prepare so that the two team members outside the office door and the four other colleagues in the office are ready for a visit from the fee earner.

Even if none of his colleagues takes his warning seriously, and none of them is concerned about what might happen, he still needs to act self-protectively.

He needs to find out what has happened to the consignment of report covers and have them to hand. Then he needs to make two inter-connected decisions: should he stay in the room or leave until the coast is clear? What should he do with the report covers?

He could decide to leave the office in which case he could take the report covers up to the fee earner's office and leave them with his PA. Or he could decide to leave the office but put the report covers prominently on his own desk and so that the fee earner sees them when he arrives. But, if he decides to stay in the office he needs to be prepared to take action as soon as the fee earner enters the room. Whatever strategy or combination of strategies he selects, he needs to take control and do something. The very act of making a decision to act in his own best interests by protecting himself alters his energy. It means that he moves from being passive to being energised; from being an easy target to being challenging to attack.

What measures could the helpdesk technician have taken during the second face-to-face attack to put the issues back to the bully? As soon as the bully enters the office the helpdesk technician needs to:

- *Get to his feet, move out from behind his desk, square his shoulders and look the fee earner firmly in the eye.* This non-verbal challenge will send the clear message back to the bully that the helpdesk technician is quite able to handle himself and ready for the fight.

- *Pre-empt his attack by handing the report covers to the fee earner with the words: 'Are these the items you are looking for?'* This strategy represents an attempt to take the ground from under the fee earner's feet before he opens his mouth. Having received the overdue report covers which he claims are the 'reason' for his anger, it would be difficult for the fee earner to proceed to a verbal tongue-lashing, although he might try to. Assuming he does, then the helpdesk technician needs to employ the next strategy as well.

- *Let the fee earner say what he wants to say and then confront him.* Using a firm tone and spacing out the words for emphasis, he could say: 'I don't believe everything you say,' or in a tone which conveys distaste he could say: 'I heard that.' These two statements achieve slightly different things for him. Let's consider each in turn.

By saying: 'I don't believe everything you say' the helpdesk technician:

- Breaks the momentum of the fee earner's rant.

- Cuts through the lies, innuendo and abuse being generated by the fee earner.

- Sends back a clear message to the fee earner that he is not intimidated and can stand his ground.

- Requires the fee earner to re-consider what he is saying.

- Makes it clear that he and he alone decides what is true and what is not: the fee earner may rage and make all kinds of accusations, but he, the helpdesk technician, is not influenced by this tirade, does not feel emotionally punctured by them, and doesn't believe them.

This latter point is crucial. The fee earner's attack on the helpdesk technician is partly about status: he thinks he is more important that the man he abuses because he brings income into the business and the helpdesk technician does not. If the technician – a man who he thinks of as an underling – knows the difference between truth and falsehood, and is prepared to say so, then what does that say about the fee earner's assumptions of superiority?

The second thing he could say, in a tone of some distaste, is: 'I heard that.' This response by the helpdesk technician:

- Lays down a clear marker that what the fee earner just said is unacceptable.

- Tells the fee earner that the helpdesk technician is listening to every word he says and evaluating it.

- Tells the fee earner that the helpdesk technician is quite in control of the situation, not at all thrown by his attack, and is using the interaction to take careful note of everything that is being said.

Both of these statements are powerful methods of interrupting an abusive flow from a workplace bully.

Let's now consider the role of the other seven members of the print media team. What could they have done to stand alongside their colleague during the second attack, and create effective consequences for the bully to deal with?

After they are physically brushed aside by the fee earner, the two colleagues chatting outside the team office have a choice to make. Are they going to ignore what has just happened to them and let the fee earner behave just as badly inside the office? Or are they going to follow him into the office and actively support their colleagues while the fee earner throws his weight around? They take the former approach, leaving their colleagues inside the room to handle the fee earner without their assistance. While we can sympathise with them to some extent – they are well-intentioned employees not used to rough and aggressive contact with colleagues – they make the wrong decision.

Both of these two colleagues need to follow the fee earner into their office, pick up a sheet of paper and in full view of the abusive fee earner start to take notes. They need to look at the clock, make a note of the time on the piece of paper, and start to write down particulars of what is occurring. The very act of doing this will give the bully something to think about. He has bullied people in the firm for years. No one in the hierarchy above him holds him accountable for his abusiveness. To date, no one has made a compliant for workplace bullying against him. However, the fact that the two colleagues he barged past are prepared to take notes contemporaneous to an assault, will give him pause for thought. He may *feel* invincible. But he is not. The two colleagues don't necessarily have to make a complaint - something which would be time-consuming, fraught with challenge and energy sapping - but they do need to look as if they might do.

The team secretary also has a choice to make. Will she give in to the shock and terror she feels when the fee earner sticks his face into hers and demands to know where the useless idiot he spoke to is? Or will she stand her ground? If she simply gives way, and indicates with a nod of her head the desk where the helpdesk technician is seated, she places her colleague in jeopardy and lays herself open to future attack: the fee earner now knows she will be an easy person to target too. How could she have sent the fee earner the message that she knows how to protect herself and her colleague?

The team secretary is standing up near the door when the fee earner enters the room. As soon as the fee earner sticks his face into hers and demands to know where the useless idiot he spoke to is seated, the team secretary needs to act. She needs to step smartly backwards, physically and metaphorically putting space between herself and the fee earner. Taking a smart step backwards tells him that he can try and physically intimidate her by putting his face into hers, but she can just as swiftly counter by stepping out of the way. Once she is a step away from him, she needs to say either: 'I would prefer you leave the office and come back when you are ready to have a business discussion' or: 'There are no useless idiots in this office.' Let's consider the different merits of these two statements.

By saying 'I would prefer you leave the office and come back when you are ready to have a business discussion' the team secretary will:

- Assert her right to decide how people behave in her office.

- Hold the fee earner accountable for his rage and abusiveness.

- Make a clear distinction between his current behaviour – aggressive and bullying – and normal business conduct.

- Tell the fee earner that she isn't intimidated by his behaviour.

- Clarify that he can rage if he wants, but she isn't going to put up with it.

- Give him a clear choice: behave in a usual business manner or go away.

The fee earner will not like hearing this message at all, but he will have to take it seriously. How he responds next will be a telling comment on his character. He could try and escalate matters, perhaps by telling her that he is more important than her or matters more to the firm. In which case she could counter with: 'That may well be true, but you are in my office', a fact which again asserts her right to a say in how people in her office behave. It is, however, much more likely that when faced with the poise and resolve of any of these retorts the abusive fee earner will simply back down, with ill grace and more aggression perhaps, but back down nonetheless. At that point, any member of the team could pick up the report covers, approach him with them and hand them to him, and using a cool tone slowly say: 'Are these the items you are shouting about?' This succinct and pithy put down would call him firmly to account. He would be faced with the fact that he uses egregious aggression at work on the pretext of a set of report covers. Seeing himself in this light will not be easy for him.

Let's now turn to the second statement which the team secretary could make. By saying: 'There are no useless idiots in this office' the team secretary will achieve something slightly different. She will:

- Hold the fee earner accountable for his insulting language.

- Break his momentum, requiring him to find something else to say.

- Put the issues firmly back to him.

- Take control of the situation.

This last point is crucial. It is quite possible that the fee earner will be so thrown by this simple and factual response that he is unable to find anything else to say. Many bullies use their targets' fear and anxiety as fuel for their attacks. If there is no evidence of either fear or anxiety, there is no fuel for the attack and many of them simply go quiet.

Finally, let's turn to the options available to the other team members in the print media team office. What could each of them have done to stand alongside the helpdesk technician during the second attack, and create effective consequences for the bully to deal with?

There are three other team members in the room at the time of the face-to-face attack on the helpdesk technician, in addition to the team secretary and the two colleagues outside the room. Each of these three people has a decision to make as well. Each of them needs to ask themselves what role they will play in the unfolding events: will they be passive enablers of the attack or active participants who confront the abuse?

Avoiding their responsibility to support the helpdesk technician is not a wise choice for any of the other three colleagues to make. It may *appear* to be self-preserving and sensible from their point of view in that it doesn't draw the fee earner's attention to the fact that they are in the room. But it is a dangerous stance to take because it tells the bully that any of them would be a soft target for future attack. Avoiding their responsibility to support the helpdesk technician increases the likelihood that the fee earner will target one of them for a future attack, as well as making them passive enablers of the attack on the helpdesk technician.

Each of the three team members in the office needs to do *something* to signal to the fee earner that they will not stand by and watch one of their team mates being abused. They could:

- *Stand up, walk towards the helpdesk technician and stand behind him:* this would tell the fee earner that the target isn't alone and has their support, that there are several of them standing together and only one of him.

- *Pick up the telephone, dial a number and say loudly into the receiver that there is an abusive incident occurring at that moment in the print media room.* The number they dial is unimportant: it could be their own home or mobile answer phone. It's the fact of actually saying these words out loud that matters. This action will turn the tide at the time of the attack. It will give the bully something to think about. It will send health-giving support to the helpdesk technician at the time of the attack, support which will bolster him and mitigate some or all of the emotional overwhelm which he would otherwise experience. It will send a clear message to the bully that he is not easily going to prevail, that he is up against people who are well able to defend themselves, that they have called for assistance, and that they will create consequences for him to deal with if he doesn't desist.

Each of the effective strategies open to the helpdesk technician, the two colleagues outside the office, the team secretary, and each of the other three team members is straightforward to enact. Each simply requires one decision: to take an active stand and put the issues back to the bully. The fact that each of these characters is prepared to do something to put the issues back to the bully sends the clear message that the bully is NOT in control of their behaviour. They are. And that message alone alters the dynamic between them powerfully in their favour.

> **Consider replacing the receiver if you are subject to abuse on the telephone.**

> **Say: 'I don't believe everything you say' or 'I heard that' to confront verbal abuse.**

> **Take a step backwards if a bully threatens you by standing physically too close to you.**

> **Creating just consequences for the bully to think about will halt their momentum during an attack.**

Exercise 3: Altering Your Behaviour at the Time of an Attack

You may now want to re-visit the incident you analysed during exercise 2 on page 121. I'd like you to look at that incident with fresh eyes. Complete the diagram below but this time make a decision about how you would like to handle the dynamics differently and better should a similar incident occur.

Start by completing the middle box. Write down behaviour you would like to use at the time of the attack. What will you do and say? When will you do and say these things? Where will you physically locate yourself when you use this behaviour?

Next, I'd like you to complete the third box to capture a realistic outcome you would like from the attack. How will it end? In what way is this different from the way the real incident ended? What will you do after it has ended?

Lastly, I'd like you to complete the first box, this time writing down A New Perspective about you and your situation at work so that you set yourself up for using the effective behaviour you have detailed in the middle box should you need to.

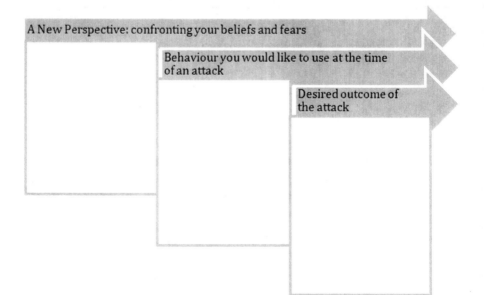

You may now want to compare this set of responses with those you gave earlier in Diagram 2 of the chapter. In particular, notice what has changed in your behaviour and how that has created different and better outcomes for you, and enabled you to think more truthful and accurate thoughts about yourself.

Summary of Key Points from the Chapter

Being subject to workplace bullying can create a level of emotional overwhelm which affects you for hours, days or weeks afterwards. Trying to make sense of what happened to you during the attack – in other words processing emotional overwhelm - can be energy sapping, confusing and disorienting. The good news is that it doesn't have to be like this. Learning how to put the issues back to the bully at the time of the attack will mitigate or prevent emotional overwhelm, leaving you free to carry on with your day.

The very fact that you decide to put the issues back to the bully moves you out of a submissive, compliant stance and into an active and engaged stance. This in and of itself alters the balance between you and the bully. However, successfully putting the issues back to the bully – creating consequences for them to handle in the moment of an attack – has the added benefit of dealing with the bullying then and there *on an emotional level.* That incident is over. You have protected yourself, handled the bullying interaction effectively and sent back a message to the bully that they can try and bully you, but you have got the measure of that situation.

Using a different behaviour at the time of the attack will change the way that the interaction plays out between you. It will influence the outcome of the encounter in your favour. Then you can go back and re-evaluate what you think, fear and believe about yourself that has left you vulnerable to being bullied.

There are many strategies you can use:

- Taking a step back from a bully who is trying to intimidate you by standing physically close to you.

- Standing up and crossing your arms when the bully enters your office or approaches you.

- Telling them that you want them to commit their complaints about you to paper so you can discuss them with your manger.

- Playing their abusive words straight back to them in the form of a statement, for instance: 'There are no idiots here.'

- Stating what you require of them: 'I would prefer you leave the office and come back when you are ready to have a business discussion.'

- Responding to a personal insult by clarifying that in your office you call the shots: 'It may well be true that I have less influence than you, but this is my office.'

- Saying 'I heard that' or 'I don't believe everything you say' to confront verbal abuse.

All of these responses send back the clear message to the bully that their attempt to intimidate you is not working, they are NOT in control of your behaviour even though they'd like to be. You are.

Questions for You to Consider

You may now like to identify a situation in which you were targeted at work. Bring a specific situation to mind and then answer the following questions about it. You can jot down your answers to each of the questions in the space below it:

1. What was the situation? What happened during it?

2. What behaviour did you use at the time? How did this approach affect the outcome of that encounter?

3. Looking back on it now, what could you have said or done differently that would have worked and swung the balance of the encounter more in your favour?

Next Chapter

Chapter 6 focuses on the issues involved when a workplace bully targets someone with more organisational authority than them, be it their line manager or another senior figure.

Chapter 6
When Your Performance is Called into Question

Responding Effectively Under Pressure

Receiving Negative Feedback from Your Manager

If you have experience of a negative evaluation of your work from your non-bullying line manager, you will recognise how challenging it can be to respond to. This situation begs many questions, especially if you feel anxious about your job as a result of the feedback or simply don't agree with it. You may wonder whether some or all of the unfavourable feedback you have received is more a reflection of your manager's different work values than it is a reflection of true shoddiness on your part. You may ask yourself whether you really deserve the degree of criticism which your manager levels at you or whether a relative lack of skill at giving developmental feedback has resulted in them overstating the case. These are issues which many of you may have grappled with during your time at work, issues which require you to:

- Step back from the feedback and your feelings about it.

- Evaluate the feedback for fact and relevance.

- Compare your outputs with your key performance indicators.

- Make a judgement about the validity of the messages you heard from your manager.

- Relay your conclusions to your manager, making it clear that you want to address any areas of true under-performance on your part.

If your energy levels are high and you feel competent at your job, these are pretty straightforward tasks, even if they are tasks you'd rather not have to invest time in doing.

But it gets more complicated if you are subject to workplace bullying. If you have direct experience of being bullied, you will recognise how challenging it can be to go to work every day, knowing that the bully may launch another attack on you. You recognise how taxing it can be to keep your mind on your work, concentrate on your tasks and *be present in the workplace* when, at any minute, you may be subject to abuse. In these circumstances, it is no wonder that your performance level drops and can become a topic for discussion with your manager.

Your manager may be unaware that you are being bullied, or may be aware of the fact of it but *not know what it means to you*. Perhaps the bully is from another department and only bullies you one-to-one when your manager is not present. Perhaps they are a patient or relative of a patient; or a customer or client whom you cannot avoid if you are to do your job effectively. Your manager may simply not understand the impact your experiences have on you, not understand the pressure you are subject to and be disappointed that your performance is not where it used to be. From their perspective, you used to be a top performer and now you aren't. From their perspective, the onus is on them to step in and invest their precious time in getting you up to speed again.

Perhaps more challenging still is the situation where the bully *is your line manager,* who now has the gall to critique you for under-performing. You hear their criticisms, feel bewildered at their duplicity, and feel floored by the tactic of attacking you for under-performing when it is their actions towards you that have rendered you unable to perform. Their campaign has moved from bullying you to using your understandable under-performance as another excuse to bully you.

This chapter explores how to handle these knotty issues should you be unfortunate enough to need to set the record straight. It provides input and direction for those of you who cannot produce work to the standard you want because much of your energy is going inwards to cope with your experience of workplace bullying. The chapter is primarily written for three distinct groups of people:

- Those of you whose excellent performance is being unfairly questioned by a key workplace contact – perhaps a colleague from another department, a team member, patient or client - as part of their campaign of workplace bullying against you.

- Those of you who used to perform effectively but, as a result of being bullied by a key workplace contact are now unable to work to the same high standards, and are faced with the fact that your lowered performance is getting you into trouble with your line manager.

- Those of you who used to produce work of a good standard before you were bullied by your own manager, and now need to face the fact that your cunning boss uses your lowered performance level as an excuse to bully you further.

However, before we examine how to handle these issues, I'd like to make a distinction between those of you in the three groups above and a fourth set of people: those who intentionally under-perform, don't want to do anything about that fact, get justified negative feedback from their manager for their below par outputs, and handle the anxiety they feel at doing a poor job by claiming that they are being bullied. Consider the following short example.

Intentional Under-Performance

- A waitress in a busy restaurant tells her boss that she is rushed off her feet and there is a pressing need for a second waiter to work alongside her in the evenings. The restaurant owner likes his employee, wants to do right by her and hires a waiter that day. The newcomer starts work the following Saturday. On his first night, he is slow to pick up empty plates from tables, gets the orders for two of the window seats mixed up, and takes a cigarette break at 8 pm in the middle of the busy period. The waitress asks him to pull his weight and he responds by shrugging his shoulders and telling her that he is doing his best.

The restaurant owner notices that the newcomer is not working as hard as his colleague and shouts at him to get into gear. The waiter complains to the waitress that the boss is an unpleasant and nasty man, and a lousy boss who yells at him. The waitress replies that while it is not right for the restaurant owner to shout at him like that, she would prefer it if the waiter made a point of refilling half of the salt and pepper pots so she can do the other half. The waiter simply stares at her with a blank expression on his face. In the silence that follows, the waitress realises that the new waiter is not at all interested in doing half the work. Over the next two weeks, the restaurant owner continues to shout at the newcomer, yelling at him to 'do the job properly.' He glares at him whenever he walks past him, his fists balled by his sides. In response, the waiter takes extra cigarette breaks, makes a point of taking orders and chatting to customers but refusing to collect dirty plates, and pockets tips instead of placing them in the communal box. As he is about to lock up on the Sunday evening, the restaurant owner calls the waiter over and fires him. Two days later, the waiter returns to the restaurant with a written complaint against the owner for workplace bullying.

In this example a waiter secures a job at a busy restaurant but has little intention of working hard. His lackadaisical attitude is apparent from the start of his employment. From early on in his employment, his laziness comes to the attention of both the restaurant owner and the waitress. The owner deals with the newcomer's intentional under-performance by shouting at him and conveying his disapproval non-verbally via glares and balled fists. The waitress deals with it by requesting that the waiter do half the work involved in filling the salt and pepper pots. Neither of these approaches influences the waiter who does not want to apply himself to the job he has accepted and is being paid to do. He is satisfied doing just enough to get by – taking orders and chatting to customers – but leaves tasks he finds more onerous, like collecting dirty plates, to his co-worker the waitress. Eventually, after shouting at him repeatedly to 'do the job properly' the restaurant owner has had enough and sacks the newcomer. Unfortunately for him, the waiter decides to up the ante and makes a complaint against him for workplace bullying. Let's explore the issues.

Lack of Integrity: Underdeveloped People-Handling Skills

Both the restaurant owner and the waiter are responsible for mishandling their interactions with one another, but in quite different ways. Let's start by taking a look at the issues in the life of the waiter.

The waiter is a work-shy and irresponsible man. He is quite comfortable accepting payment for a job he does less than adequately, and is able to square that set of circumstances with his conscience. From the start of his employment, he does less of the work than his colleague the waitress. He cherry-picks tasks he likes – chatting to customers, taking orders – and leaves the tasks he doesn't like so much - like collecting dirty plates and filling salt and pepper pots - to his colleague to do by herself. The waiter justifies his laziness to himself quite easily. He does this by telling himself he is doing the best he can and by blaming his boss who he quickly decides is unpleasant and nasty. While it is true that the restaurant owner lacks people-handling skills, he is neither nasty nor unpleasant. He simply wants his employee to do the work he is being paid to do. Accusing him of workplace bullying is an unjustified attempt to try it on by a short-term employee who wants to see if he can take more money he hasn't earned and isn't entitled to from the owner of the restaurant.

Let's now turn to the issues in the life of the restaurant owner. The restaurant owner is a harassed and well-intentioned man who lacks people-skills. He recognises that there is too much work for the waitress to do by herself, and acts swiftly when she asks him to hire an additional waiter. But he makes a poor choice, allowing his urgent need for a second employee to colour his judgement. He hires the first person he meets without finding out enough about him. He regrets his decision very quickly, but lacking the influencing or conflict-resolution skills he needs to address the problem, he makes a bad situation worse. He shouts at his new recruit and is non-verbally aggressive towards him, actions which only harden the waiter's resolve to do as little as possible for as long as he can. The restaurant owner recognises that his new recruit has not responded positively to being shouted at and is still not pulling his weight. But instead of talking to him constructively, he repeats his error. He yells at him again and again, ordering him to 'do the job properly.' Every time he yells at him, the waiter reacts by doing even less work. Eventually, the restaurant owner accepts that he has made a poor choice in hiring the waiter and decides to cut his losses. He sacks him summarily and fully expects that the matter will end there. He is surprised to see the waiter again two days later and even more surprised that the waiter brings with him a complaint for workplace bullying.

The central question is: does the restaurant owner allow his frustration at the half-hearted work being done by the waiter to result in workplace bullying? No, he does not. Let's refer to the three-part definition in Chapter 1 to find out why. The restaurant owner is not a bully for three reasons:

- He has *not tried to remove power* from the waiter; but sought to influence him towards better performance.

- He has *not set out to injure the waiter emotionally or psychologically nor has he tried to render him unable to do his job competently*; in fact he tried to get him to do his job more effectively no matter how unskilfully he tackled this challenge.

- While he did repeatedly shout at the waiter who did not like being yelled at, his bawling at him was *not emotionally hurtful or professionally harmful* to the waiter; in fact the waiter treated being yelled at as a pretext to do even less work.

Overall, while we can sympathise with the restaurant owner's frustration that his new recruit is not performing effectively, we can also say that the restaurant owner is in serious need of learning how to recruit effectively, how to manage people skilfully and how to handle his own frustration more maturely. While he needs to learn that yelling at a member of staff is neither motivating nor influential, he is not a workplace bully.

Equally, we can say that the waiter is in serious need of applying himself to the job he is paid to do. From the moment he accepts employment with the restaurant owner he intentionally under-performs. He needs to demonstrate the integrity which would enable him to do a fair day's work for a fair day's pay, and if he decides that he does not like a particular job, he still needs to do it as well as he can while seeking different employment. Both of these characters need to learn from their mistakes if they are to avoid repeating the same patterns of behaviour in similar circumstances.

The Challenge of Managing People

Managing people is a job that requires a specific skill-set if the incumbent is to perform it effectively. Managers need a range of people-handling, influencing and conflict-resolution skills which enable them to engage and work productively with members of staff:

- With whom they have nothing in common, no shared values and different ways of working.

- With whom they get on well and have similar workplace priorities, but to whom they must not show favouritism.

- Who occasionally or consistently under-perform or who struggle to maintain the standard of work the manager expects.

In the above example, the restaurant manager doesn't possess the skills he needs to make a sound judgement about the work-ethic or aptitude of a new hire, doesn't possess the influencing or feedback skills he needs to motivate his recruit to produce higher work standards, and ends up firing him. The issues in this example are quite clear cut. But what about a more complicated example, one which involves a well-intentioned but averagely skilled manager and an employee in his team who is being bullied by a customer? For the purposes of the following case study its central character, a care home nurse, does not know how to respond effectively to bullying behaviour.

Case Study 4: Bullying Customer

A nurse accepts employment in a small care home for elderly residents. She joins a team of six nurses. She reports to the care home owner, a well-intentioned but limited manager, who also runs a small hotel and a number of take away businesses. Each nurse is assigned to a number of specific patients and the new nurse finds that she is so busy she has limited time to interact with the other nurses. Nonetheless, she enjoys her job, builds close and affectionate bonds with her patients, and is happy working for the care home owner who trusts her to get on with the work without needing much input from him.

Two years into her employment, the nurse becomes subject to workplace bullying from the husband of an elderly resident. The husband is a physically big man, tall and imposing. He arranges for his wife to become a resident at the care home, and tells the nurse that he has taken this step to ensure that she gets the care she deserves. The nurse is assigned to nurse her. Her new patient has a number of complicated, inter-connected medical conditions but responds well to the nurse's personalised service and genuine empathy for her distress at being largely confined to her bed. They get on well, and the patient starts to open up to the nurse about her husband's brusque and hard manner. The husband is displeased to notice the growing bond between the two women and, at the end of one of his visits to see her, determines to act.

He approaches the nurse at her desk in the front hallway, stands silently in front of her and waits for her to look up from her paperwork. She raises her head, smiles at him and asks him how his wife seems that day. He responds by telling her in a brusque and cold tone that he is unimpressed that water has been allowed to seep into the bedclothes at the bottom of his wife's bed. He demands that she 'sort it out immediately.' The nurse is thrown. She has no idea how water could have ended up on her patient's bed. The patient herself is too weak to hold a cup of water to her lips – the nurse does this for her – and is unlikely to have thrown water all over the bottom of the bed. The nurse cannot account for what might have happened. Nonetheless, she rushes upstairs, enters her patient's room and is dismayed to find water all over her bedclothes.

The following day she receives a curt handwritten note from the husband informing her that he will be visiting the home that afternoon. The nurse reads the note and frowns. She does not understand why the husband would write to inform her that he will be coming to see his wife in advance of doing so. She puts the letter down to a quirk of his personality and deposits it in her desk drawer. She thinks no more about it. The husband does indeed arrive later that day and once more takes the time to bully the nurse. He is personally rude to her face, referring to her as 'the menial who looks after my wife.' From that point onwards, every time he visits he makes a point of intimidating the nurse. He criticises her work, pointing out a supposed flaw or failing in the way his wife's room or bedclothes have been arranged, while also making personal and offensive remarks to the nurse or about her in her hearing. The nurse is a kind and accommodating character unused to such aggression. She feels hurt and confused by the actions of the husband of a patient she cares for very much. She handles his offensive remarks by telling herself that he is worried about his wife, under pressure because he is apart from her and doesn't really mean it. Then she leaves the room and carries on with her work.

Finally, two months into the husband's campaign of bullying her, the care home manager asks to see the nurse during one of his infrequent visits to the care home. He calls the nurse into his office, asks her to sit down and pulls a folder out from his briefcase. He seems tense and edgy. He tells her that he has received a number of letters of complaint from the husband of one of her patients, the contents of which have concerned him greatly. He tells her that the husband is so worried about the 'planned neglect' that he has observed perpetrated against his wife at the care home, that he is considering reporting the nurse to the Royal College of Nursing for misconduct. He reads the letter to her and tells the nurse that he is taking the contents of the letters seriously. He informs her that her role is now under review.

Analysing the Dynamics in Case Study 4: Bullying Customer

In this example, a good natured care home nurse is subject to a campaign of workplace bullying from the husband of one of her patients. She is an easy target for the bully: she cares about his wife, does not know how to defend herself against his bullying, lacks day-to-day support from her pleasant but distant nursing colleagues, and rarely sees her boss who is busy with his other businesses. The campaign of bullying which the husband orchestrates against her includes the following elements:

- Pouring water onto his wife's bedclothes when he is in her room alone with her, something for which he subsequently blames the nurse.

- Sending her a confusing letter simply to see how she handles it.

- Making personally offensive remarks to the nurse whenever he speaks with her.

- Speaking about her in a derogatory manner behind her back, but while she is in ear-shot and can hear him.

- Writing a number of letters of complaint to the care home owner without the nurse's knowledge, in which he details a series of fabricated allegations against her.

- Threatening to report the nurse for planned negligence to her professional body the Royal College of Nursing.

Let's explore the issues. We will begin by looking inside the life of the husband to identify the factors in him which create the impulse to bully. Then we will examine the issues in the nurse's life that render her vulnerable to attack, before highlighting what she needs to do to set the record straight with her boss and keep her job.

Deflecting Attention, Creating a Scapegoat

The husband is an unloving and cruel man whose dislike of, and antipathy towards his wife, contributes to her interconnected medical conditions. His decision to place her in a care home is not about wanting her to receive better care than he could provide at home, although that is how he presents it. It is about his wish to remove her from his house so he doesn't have to live with her anymore. He wants to continue his vendetta against his wife when she is in the care home, so he selects a small home near to his house, and makes sure that it has a largely absent owner who leaves the day-to-day care to his staff members.

On his early visits to the care home, the husband portrays himself as a conscientious and concerned spouse. During each of his early visits he observes that his wife and her nurse get on well, and the growing bond between them concerns him. He does not want his wife to inform her nurse about how nasty he has been to her throughout their marriage. He decides to take measures to prevent this possibility from occurring. The husband is pleased to note the sensitive and thoughtful demeanour of the nurse and decides to target her in an attempt to dissuade her from speaking about him. He tests how susceptible she might be by grooming her. He pours water over his wife's bedclothes while in the room with her alone, so that he can then go downstairs and complain to the nurse about it. He observes how the nurse handles this unexpected incident, recognises her confusion and vulnerability, and decides to groom her again.

This time he sends her a letter informing her of his arrival later that day. This is a warning note, and it is a warning that the nurse does not recognise. When she neither asks him why he wrote it nor changes her outward demeanour toward him as a result of reading it, the husband realises that he is unlikely to receive much resistance from her. He swiftly proceeds to a campaign of bullying. He insults the nurse whenever he meets her, calls her by derogatory names and criticises her work. The nurse offers no resistance to these tactics, and mentally puts them down to his stress levels. Over the next few weeks, the husband starts to send fabricated allegations to the care home manager in a planned assault upon the nurse's reputation and credibility. He refers to the nurse's supposed actions towards his wife as 'planned negligence' and threatens to report her to the RCN. Why would he act in such a despicable way?

The husband takes these steps because he has something to hide. His decision to move his wife out of his house backfires on him when she forms a close bond with her nurse. The husband becomes afraid that his wife may start to tell her nurse about the years of passive and active abuse she has experienced at the hands of her husband. He bullies the nurse to intimidate her into remaining quiet, while simultaneously destroying her credibility with her employer and professional body through a series of fabricated allegations. He takes both of these steps to deflect attention away from his own wrongdoing. Better to damage the reputation of the nurse in advance so that no one will believe her should she decide to report him to the authorities. The husband lays a trap for the nurse and executes a cold and calculating plan.

Let's now turn our attention towards the nurse to identify firstly, the factors in her life which render her vulnerable to a particularly malicious campaign of workplace bullying; and secondly, the steps open to her to turn the tables on the husband, retain her job and avoid being unjustly reported to the RCN.

The Risk of Ignoring Red Flags

The nurse is an excellent nurse, and a dedicated and caring woman. But she has two areas for development which she has not attended to in her life, areas which render her vulnerable to the calculating abuse of the husband. The first is that she hates conflict and avoids it whenever she can. The second is that she is not a good judge of character, preferring not to look too closely at the lives of those around her. She completely misses the motives of the husband and initially excuses his offensive remarks towards her, wrongly attributing them to his stress levels. She allows these two areas for development to *cloud her judgement about the circumstances surrounding her patient and the patient's husband.* Let's see how these two areas for development contribute to her plight.

The nurse eschews conflict. She avoids it all costs, even to the point of failing to ask the simple questions of the husband: 'when did you first notice the water on the bedclothes?' or 'what did you want to achieve by sending me this letter?' or 'why are you being rude to me?' She does not ask a question if she thinks it might provoke tension, disagreement or disharmony. She also melts away in the face of aggression, insult or rudeness. She mentally excuses the husband for being offensive to her, puts his distressing remarks down to his stress levels, and employs the strategy of removing herself from the room. This is the case even if, as with the husband's insulting words, the insult is clearly directed at her. She hears it, notes it and removes herself from the room. She has sufficient self-esteem not to be injured by rudeness – she does not take it to heart – but she does feel unsettled and confused by his verbal attacks on her. However, she does not do anything afterwards to prevent recurrence. At no point during his campaign of verbal bullying and physical intimidation against her does the nurse confront the husband, tell a colleague what is happening to her or report the husband to her manager, the care home owner. She avoids doing so and makes it easy for the husband to bully her.

Her second area for development concerns the fact that she is not a good judge of character. She lives at quite a superficial level, and is a passive participant in her day-to-day life. Although she is a caring woman, she does not look much beyond the surface of a situation. In the normal course of her work, this probably would not matter. But as soon as her work brings her into contact with the husband, it begins to matter very much indeed. The nurse builds close bonds with all the people in her care, and that is true of the connection she builds with the patient. Although she thinks the patient's husband is a rude man and a cold fish, she does not go beyond that thought. She thinks it is very odd indeed that so much water could have got onto the patient's bedclothes, but she remains passive and does not search for an answer to the question. She changes the bedclothes and moves on with her day without reporting the incident, without talking it over with any of her colleagues and without considering the obvious answer. There are only three people who could reasonably have poured the water onto the bedclothes: herself, the patient or her husband. She knows she didn't do it. She also knows that her patient isn't mobile enough or strong enough to pour water across the foot of her bed. So it has to be the husband - even though he was the one who drew her attention to it. The husband learns that when presented with a potentially confusing set of circumstances, the nurse does not protect herself by enquiring about what actually happened. She only responds practically by solving the problem. The husband makes a mental note.

Her superficial engagement with what is going on around her works against the nurse's best interests a second time when she mishandles the circumstances surrounding the handwritten letter. The husband sends her an apparently pointless letter informing her that he will be arriving later that day simply to see how the nurse reacts. Will she confront him and enquire what the letter means? Or will she let the incident slide? The nurse decides that the letter is evidence of some foible on the part of the husband and puts it in her drawer without checking it out with him. The husband takes mental note once more. The way is clear for him to move to the second part of his campaign: subjecting her to a series of humiliating verbal attacks while concocting a series of fabricated complaints about her, writing them down and posting them to her manager.

Responding to an Abusive Complaint

Finally, let's turn our attention to what the nurse needs to do to handle her meeting with her manager effectively. It is very late in the day for her to realise that she has been set up and she will need to think clearly, speak factually and handle the interview unemotionally if she is to right a wrong. Her conduct, integrity and performance are all subject to question. What can the nurse do to protect herself against slanderous, abusive allegations and right the wrong that is being perpetrated against her? Let's examine the options.

The nurse needs to see the situation for what it is: a set of fabricated allegations against her. She needs to keep uppermost in her mind the fact that the allegations consist of lies and slanders and there is no veracity to them. She needs to respond with facts. She needs to keep a level head, speak with a clear and firm voice, and let the truth speak for itself. She cannot afford to mishandle the moment. Although right is on her side, she needs to handle this meeting in the most influential and persuasive way she can, to secure a just outcome. Her manager thought well enough of her to hire her, and has trusted her – along with her nursing colleagues – to handle her duties without much assistance from him. Now he is faced with a series of allegations about her for which he has no evidence one way or the other, delivered in writing by someone he doesn't know. In order, here are the points the nurse needs to make to her manager.

In a tone which relays the following information as fact, the nurse needs to:

- *Tell her manager that she is shocked and surprised* that he has a received a series of fabricated written complaints about her from the husband.

- *Acknowledge that the letters are very difficult to listen to,* and she is concerned and disappointed that so many lies have been written about her.

- Tell him that *she cares very much for her patient,* the wife of the abusive complainant, that they have formed a strong bond, and that she is sure the patient would corroborate this fact.

- Tell him that the *husband has been difficult to deal with* from the start of his wife's stay at the home, and has regularly used insulting and offensive language when speaking with her.

- Tell him that the husband has employed a *physically intimidating and threatening demeanour* in most of his interactions with her.

- Inform him that *his wife is doing very well under her care* and has visibly picked up since being admitted to the care home.

- Ask him to *speak privately with her patient* to enquire about her satisfaction with the quality of care she has received from the nurse, making sure that this conversation occurs when the husband is not present and before he knows it is to take place.

- Ask him to work with her to make sure that the *needs of her patient* are given high priority going forward.

- *Ask him a series of questions* including: if you had not received these letters, what would be your opinion of my work? What do you value most about me as an employee and as a nurse? What do you want to do as a result of receiving these letters? What would be the worst outcome for you from this situation? What would be the best outcome for you from this situation?

At this point, she needs to listen carefully to the responses her manager gives her to her questions and, assuming he is influenced by her calm and factual presentation, she could continue to set the record straight by making the following points:

- *That it is likely that the husband poured water onto his wife's bed* so he could appear to be acting in her best interests when he subsequently reported the incident to the nurse, and that this is a clear example of the way he does things.

- That she thinks he is *highly motivated to act in this way* and has put a lot of thought into the slanderous allegations he has made against her in the hope that her manager will believe them.

- That should she have to fight a second abusive complaint made to the RCN, she hopes very much that *her manager will support her.*

Put the facts on the table and let your manager make up their own mind.

Using Fact and Truth to Set the Record Straight

Let's take stock of what the nurse has achieved by handling her taxing interview with her manager this way. By handling things like this, the nurse:

- Enables her manager to make up his own mind based on the facts.

- Takes seriously the allegations against her without appearing to be crushed by them.

- Avoids the pitfall of becoming emotional in the meeting, thereby reducing the likelihood that she can defend herself effectively.

- Avoids looking to her manager for emotional support or rescue.

- Articulates the issues clearly and factually, portraying herself as conscientious, mature and responsible towards herself, the patient and her employer.

- Avoids complaining about the husband or making counter-allegations about him.

- Avoids becoming defensive about the allegations.

- Describes the seriousness of the situation she now faces in factual terms.

- Appeals to her manager's knowledge of her character and work.

- Portrays herself as someone who wants to confront the wrong doing, needs assistance to do so effectively, and is willing to work with her manager openly as he decides what to do next.

- Suggests that her manager speak with the central figure in the allegations – her patient – to find out what she thinks about the quality of care she has received, before he forms any conclusions.

- Warns him to do this without letting the husband know what he is planning in advance, and advises him to hold the conversation without the husband being present in the room.

- Portrays confidence in her own ability at a time when her work is being castigated.

This last point is crucial. By asserting her own confidence in her competence, the nurse, an honest woman, implicitly casts doubt on the validity of the allegations against her. Her manager now has a question to answer. Quite simply, he needs to decide who he believes. His choice is:

- An employee who needs little supervision, who has worked for him for two years, who builds robust and caring bonds with her patients and who is confronting the allegations against her with clarity, courage and integrity.

Or:

- The husband of a patient who has written him a series of letters, who has not been to see him about any of his concerns, who has not reported any of his concerns to the nurse herself, and who the nurse describes as rude, offensive and physically intimidating.

Put like this, it ought to be straightforward for the manager to support his employee, although the exact nature of that support is yet to be determined. Even with her manager's support, these are testing times for the nurse. She remains in a vulnerable situation should the husband decide to act on his written threat and make a complaint against her to the RCN. For any allegations against her to be proved groundless during an investigation by her professional body, it is important that the patient give a favourable report of the nurse's care, testimony which could sway the case against her.

Lowered Performance: a Consequence of Workplace Bullying

So far, we have been discussing the issues you might face when your effective performance is unjustly called into question by a bullying workplace contact as part of their campaign against you. Let's now turn to a different scenario and simultaneously examine what happens when:

- As a result of being bullied at work, you are unable to produce your usual high standards of work and consequently get into trouble with your line manager due to your lowered performance.

And:

- You are being bullied by your manager, who then uses your consequent lowered performance as an excuse to bully you further.

Consider the following separate, but connected, short examples:

- During a major overhaul of the technology platform in the museum where he works, a mild-mannered curator is subject to workplace bullying from the museum's head of IT. The two colleagues need to work closely together on the project and, since it was at his request that the mainframe overhaul was commissioned, the curator feels he has to continue to meet one-to-one with the head of IT. The head technologist is the more robust of the two characters, forceful and energetic. He despises the more understated and considered style of his colleague, thinking him insubstantial and lacking in confidence, a combination of traits he finds intolerable. He bullies him, using their values difference as a pretext for the campaign. As a result of being bullied, the standard of the curator's work for his line manager declines and his lowered performance comes to the attention of his manager. Unable to face the fact that he is being bullied by someone he admires for his energy and drive, the curator tells his manager that he hasn't been feeling well for some time, will go and see his doctor, and will get back into gear quickly. Two weeks later, his manager has not detected any improvement in his team member's work. In fact, two of the curator's team colleagues have complained to him that *they* have had to step in and pick up some of the curator's work, actions which are compromising their own workloads. Thoroughly fed up at what he sees as the curator's careless approach to his duties, the manager calls the curator into his office. He tells him that enough is enough. He berates the curator for 'letting your work fall onto the shoulders of your colleagues' and 'for taking me for a fool.'

- In addition to bullying the curator, the head of IT at the museum starts to bully one of his team members. The team member reports directly to him. She is well regarded by her team colleagues for her methodical, precise and thorough approach to her duties. Her work is usually of a very high standard but is often a few days late, a fact which, before he started to bully her, the head of IT regularly drew to her attention. The head of IT decides that his work at the museum is a little dull in comparison to the high octane environment of banking where he used to work. He decides to create some additional excitement for himself by bullying his quality conscious but measured team member. He makes sure that he only bullies her in their daily private one-to-one meetings, and is scrupulously careful to make tea or coffee for her at least once a day in full view of her colleagues in the open plan office. During their one-to-one meetings, his tone and style of dealing with her are aggressive and unreasonable. He complains loudly about her habit of missing deadlines. He uses an irritated and dismissive tone to belittle her. He uses withering rebukes to put down her well-intentioned but unwise explanations about why her work is often a few days late. He criticises and questions her application and the level of effort she puts into her work, and ridicules her by asking her if she wouldn't be better off working somewhere more predictable and structured than his department. Three weeks after the start of his campaign of bullying, the female team member feels anxious and sick each morning as she prepares to leave for work. During the day, she feels tired and lethargic. She finds it difficult to concentrate. The pace of her work slows down even more and, in an attempt to avoid taking further criticism from her manager, she decides not to attend the one-to-one meeting with him which is scheduled for that afternoon. This strategy backfires when, at the start of the following day, the head of IT approaches her desk and tells her that he wants her to attend an urgent formal review of her work which he has scheduled for two o'clock that day.

In the first example, a well-intentioned manager does not recognise that his team member, a museum curator, is being bullied by the head of IT. He is unaware that his team member's lowered performance is often a consequence of being abused in his workplace. He decides that a simple discussion about the need to up his game will put his errant team member back on track and enable him to perform to standard again. During this conversation, the curator cannot find it in himself to admit to his manager that he is being bullied. He feels ashamed that the head of IT characterises him as weak and inadequate, and does not want to talk about it with his boss. Instead of telling his manager that he is being bullied, he tells him a half-truth while simultaneously making an excuse. He says he hasn't been feeling well, will go to his doctor and will perform better in future. These three statements are all true. He *hasn't* been feeling well. He *will* go and see his doctor. And he *does* want to perform to his usual high standards. But the fact is: *he is being bullied,* something which he omits to mention. As long as the campaign against him continues unchallenged, it will be very difficult for him to find the reserves of energy he requires to perform as effectively as he used to. During the following two weeks, he does not manage to improve his performance. He continues to perform at a lower standard than required and subsequently receives the annoyance of his manager who wrongly concludes that the curator is deliberately letting his 'work to fall onto the shoulders of your colleagues' while also taking him 'for a fool.' The curator now has to handle a bully who is making his life at work miserable, the irritation of team members fed up at having to do aspects of his work, and the unhelpful and inaccurate conclusions that his manager has come to about him.

In the second example, the same workplace bully decides to target a second colleague, a member of his own team. He decides to target a reserved, analytical, hardworking member of his team in order to add some much-needed spice into his working routine. He is careful to attack her only during their daily one-to-one meetings, and to make a point of being 'nice' to her in front of the rest of the team, making her tea or coffee every day to create the impression that he is supportive towards her. His castigating criticisms of her have the desired effect and unsurprisingly, her performance levels fall. The head of IT pounces. He swiftly sets up a formal review of her work, using the museum's performance management processes as an avenue through which to inflict further bullying on his team member.

Responding Effectively to a Non-Bullying Manager

In these two related but quite different examples, a curator and an IT team member need to give an account to their manager for why their performance standards have lowered in recent weeks. Both of them are subject to bullying behaviour. The curator's manager simply does not know that his team member is being abused by the head of IT and wrongly concludes that he is taking him for a fool. The IT team member is being bullied by her line manager, the head of IT, who then uses her lowered performance as a pretext for bullying her for under-performing. How should these two colleagues proceed? Let's start with the curator.

In his meeting with his annoyed manager, the curator needs to make a direct distinction between:

- What his manager *thinks* is behind his lowered performance.

And:

- What is *actually* behind his lowered performance.

This is a critical distinction for him to make. His manager has already quite wrongly concluded that the curator doesn't care about his work, doesn't care that his colleagues are picking up some of his work for him, and doesn't care about the impact of his lowered performance on his manager. Imagine the frustration of his well-intentioned manager who discovers that the curator is under-performing and apparently uncommitted to improving the quality of his work. Imagine the strain on the manager who has taken his under-achieving team member through the detail of what to do differently and better, who has invested time and effort in this way, and who still cannot see any sustained performance improvement in the curator's work. Imagine the challenges facing the manager when he becomes subject to questions from his own bosses about why certain tasks being performed by the curator are not done at all or are not to standard. How does the manager justify his failure to influence the curator towards higher work quality? What exactly does he tell his bosses? Does he say: 'I have already told him' and risk appearing incompetent? Does he say: 'I'm pulling my hair out too!' and risk appearing powerless? Or does he say: 'I am still on to it' and risk appearing ineffectual? These are the issues facing the curator's line manager when he confronts his team member for intentionally letting his team colleagues pick up his work and for taking him for a fool.

In his meeting with his manager, the curator needs to set the record straight in simple, clear, factual terms. He needs to say that:

- He *wants very much to perform to his usual level,* and is very aware that he is not doing so.

- He is *not at all comfortable that his team colleagues are picking up his work*, and he is *not trying to make a fool* out of his manager.

- The *conclusions that his manager has come to about him are understandable* given the information he has available to him but his manager *does not have the whole story.*

- The crucial piece of information his manager lacks is that he, the curator, *is being bullied at work.*

At this point, the curator needs to take a breath. This achieves two things for him. Firstly, it gives him a moment to collect himself which he needs to do because, up until now, he has not wanted to speak with his manager about the fact that he is being bullied at work, and he needs to find the courage to do so now. Secondly, it gives his manager time to process what he is being told. This is important because the manager is angry at the start of the meeting. He thinks he is being ill-used by his team member, and his emotions are running high. He needs time to calm down, digest the new information, make sense of it, recognise the validity of it and then return to his dialogue with the curator. Only at this point can the two of them work in concert to find a way forward.

Having told his manager he is being bullied, and given them both time to reflect, the curator can now go onto the front foot. There are a number of ways he could structure the remainder of the meeting. Let's take a look at three options:

- The curator could focus the next part of the meeting around gauging the level of support his manager may extend to him as he decides how to handle being bullied. To do this effectively, he needs a clear view about the level of trust that exists between him and his manager, and the quality of connection his manager has with the bully. He could decide to name the bully, or not. He could simply put the fact of being bullied on the table without naming the bully, and wait to see what his manager says next. Even if his manager responds supportively, the curator may still decide to handle his situation in a guarded way. He could decide not to name the bully directly, but instead suggest that his preference would be for him to take a colleague with him to future meetings with the head of IT. This approach lets his manager fill in the blanks.

- The curator could focus the next part of the meeting around his frayed relationships with his team members. He could suggest that he talk with his team colleagues himself and thank them for picking up his work. He might tell his manager that he wants to do this himself so he can acknowledge the service his team mates have done him, and re-establish open dialogue with each of them.

- The curator could address the issues created for his manager by his under-performance. He needs to find out what these issues are in specific terms, and demonstrate that he would like to do what he can to make redress. He may want to offer his manager the option of accompanying him to the next meeting he has with *his* managers, so that the curator can give these senior figures an update on where he has got to with his work. This is a supportive way of relieving his manager of the task of explaining on his behalf, but it would require that the curator feels sufficiently confident to take part in a senior meeting. The benefit to his manager is that this is a direct method of taking responsibility for having let him down through under-performing, albeit while being bullied. Of course, the curator can only do this if he feels able to take on the task of presenting his work to the manager's bosses. It would not be a wise thing to undertake unless he feels he will be able to handle the meeting effectively. Given that he is being bullied, it may well be a step too far. But if he can manage it, it would be an effective strategy for him to use to repair his relationship with his manager.

However, the curator may decide that enough is enough. He may decide that he is being so injured by repeated bullying that he needs time away from work, and that the meeting with his manager at which his performance is being called into question is a suitable forum at which to say so. He could simply put his need for a break from work due to workplace bullying on the table and observe how his manager responds before making the other decisions outlined above.

Whichever route the curator decides to take it is important that he avoid:

- Becoming defensive, attacking his manager back: up until now, his manager is unaware that he is being bullied because the curator has hidden the fact from him.

- Complaining that his manager does not understand how much effort the curator has put into his work at a time of great pressure: the fact is that his work is of a lower standard than usual, and trying to justify himself won't work in his favour.

- Suggesting that his manager is being unfair on him: resisting his manager's feedback will not serve the curator's best interests and will add to his manager's concerns about him.

- Expecting his manager to rescue him from the bully: something which is not strictly possible.

- Expecting his manager to offer him emotional support: should his manager prove sympathetic and *offer* empathy that would be great, but the curator will only set himself up for more hurt if he expects this response from his manager. It is more likely that his manager will want to confine himself to the business issues between them, and the curator needs to be prepared for this possibility.

Even though his manager is a well-intentioned man, the curator will need to find the courage to tell him that, unpalatable though it is, he is being bullied and *this* is the reason his work standards have lowered.

> **Don't becoming defensive, justify or complain to your manager. Don't look to them for rescue or emotional support.**

Responding Effectively to a Bullying Manager

Let's now turn to the situation involving the IT team member. In this situation, the head of IT bullies his team member and then uses her lowered performance as an excuse to set up a formal review of her work under the museum's performance management processes. How should the IT team member handle this meeting?

This will be a very challenging meeting for the IT team member. The meeting involves her speaking with her abuser about the impact his abuse is having on her ability to perform. This is potentially a vulnerable environment for her to deal with. Her dual aims for the meeting need to be to:

- Protect herself as much as possible by going onto the front foot at the start, and using the facts to set the record straight.

- Turn the tables on her abuser by presenting him with a clear choice: cease bullying her or face the consequences.

The IT team member's first task is to ensure that the meeting, which is scheduled for two o'clock that day, is held in a private meeting room. She needs to be in the meeting room waiting for her manager when he arrives for the two o'clock start. She needs to be in gear and ready for him. Seated upright, and looking him in the eye from the moment he enters the room, she can start the meeting straight away by putting the facts surrounding her manager's bullying of her on the table. Employing a low-key, considered, composed style of speaking, she can proceed to outline the following facts:

- She *understands that her performance is under review* and that, alongside that conversation, she would like to have a second conversation: one about her *manager's aggressive and belittling behaviour towards her.*

- She has experienced her manager using *increasing levels of aggression* towards her in recent weeks.

- She is quite *willing to discuss her lowered performance, but only in the context of her manager's persistent, unwarranted criticisms of her style, values and demeanour,* none of which constitutes behaviour she would expect from an effective manager.

- If he is unwilling to discuss his behaviour towards her, and does not agree to cease belittling her, she will *consider going ahead with a planned complaint for workplace bullying.*

- Her research on the subject has revealed that formal complaints for workplace bullying are *time consuming, involve a forensic search for evidence, and create strain* for the party named in the complaint.

- She hopes he will change his behaviour sufficiently so that she does not have to make a complaint, but she is quite willing to do so and *will keep the option on the table for as long as she continues to report directly to him.*

She now needs to give her manager time to digest her presentation of the facts and ask him *where he would like to take the meeting next.* This way of handling things simultaneously achieves several outcomes for the IT team member. It:

- Sends a clear message to the bully that, at the moment of his greatest coup, she is quite able to turn the situation to her advantage.

- Re-frames the meeting to take back her power.

- Makes a direct link between his bullying of her and her lowered performance.

- Makes it clear that she will not let him separate the two issues.

- Presents him with a clear choice: stop bullying her or face the consequences.

- Leaves the threat of a formal complaint on the table to reinforce this point.

- Paints an unpleasant picture of the process of a formal complaint.

- Portrays herself as strong-minded, full of resolve and able to use the museum's human resources processes to *her* advantage.

- Tells the bullying manager that while he has had the upper hand so far, he has over-reached himself and needs to take note of that fact.

It is likely that the IT team member does not want to make a formal complaint for workplace bullying. This would be a time-consuming and stressful undertaking, and one which would place great strain on her. But there can be no hint of ambivalence in her demeanour as she puts the option on the table in her meeting with the bullying head of IT. She needs to handle this portion of the meeting in a way which indicates to him that she *would* be prepared to make a complaint. The head of IT is no fool. He *is* more loud, robust and vigorous than anyone else in the museum. *He is also bullying the curator.* There will be evidence of his forceful style, even if it is anecdotal. Since he is careful to bully both of his colleagues in one-to-one meetings behind closed doors, a formal complaint against him may well be not proven. Nevertheless, being subject to an investigation will not be without reputational risk for him. He now has a choice: cease bullying his team member or face the consequences.

> **Take control of the meeting. Give the bully a clear choice. Consider putting the option of a complaint on the table.**

Summary of Key Points from the Chapter

Responding effectively to negative feedback from your manager requires specific skills. When your manager is not a bully and you are committed to performing as effectively as you can, your task is pretty straightforward. You need to step back from the feedback, remain objective about it, and evaluate your performance against your key performance indicators to ascertain if the feedback is valuable to you or not.

But if the negative feedback you receive from your manager is a result of workplace bullying, a different set of skills is required.

Lowered performance is often a consequence of workplace bullying. As your energy goes inward to cope with the pressure you are under, so there is less energy available to go to your work. As your anxiety levels rise in anticipation of another attack, so it becomes difficult to concentrate and apply yourself wholeheartedly to the tasks that you are paid to handle.

Your well-intentioned, non-bullying manager may not know that you are being bullied and are subject to abuse at work. The first issue you need to confront is that, up until now, you have kept the fact of bullying from your manager. Now that your performance is being called into question, it is important that you give them this key piece of information. It may be uncomfortable for you to talk about the fact that you are being bullied with your manager, but it is vital that you challenge any assumptions they may have made about why you are working to a standard that is less effective than usual. Equally important is that you give your manager time to process the new information before you go on to discuss the issues with them. How you structure the next part of the meeting will depend on your judgement about the quality of relationship your manager has with the bully, as well as the level of support and trust between you and your manager. You may decide to name the bully, or you may not. Either way, it is important that you keep the meeting with your manager to the business issues between you, unless your manager signals that they are available to be supportive and empathic. Don't expect rescue: it is not possible for your manager to rescue you. And don't expect emotional support. If your manager does offer you support, that would be great. But expecting it could lead to disappointment if your manager doesn't feel equipped to offer you empathy. Be prepared to address the issues which your lowered performance has created for your manager as well as testing the waters to see what support they may be able to offer you.

However, if your performance is being called into question by a workplace bully as part of their campaign of bullying against you, you need to use a carefully crafted approach: that of protecting yourself as much as possible while also creating consequences for the bully to think about. An effective way to do this is to be in the meeting room before the bully arrives and take control of events straight away. Tell them that you understand that your performance is under review and that you are putting a second issue alongside that one: the second issue being that you are subject to unwarranted aggression from your manager which is affecting your performance. Make it clear that while you are quite comfortable discussing your lowered performance you only want to do this in the context of your manager's persistent, unreasonable criticisms of you, your style, your values and your work. Stay on the front foot by presenting your manager with a clear choice: cease using aggression towards you or receive a complaint for workplace bullying. Point out the consequences for your manager of being named in a formal complaint for workplace bullying: the extensive amount of time, strain and tension involved in a forensic search for evidence, with the consequent reputational risk for them. Tell your manager that you hope their behaviour towards you will alter enough that you don't have to make a complaint, but that you will keep the option on the table for as long as you work for them. Then ask your manager where they would like to take the meeting next.

Questions for You to Consider

You may now like to apply the material from this chapter to your own situation. Identify a specific situation in which you were subject to bullying behaviour at work as a result of which your performance was called into question by your manager. Answer the following questions about that situation. You can jot down your answers to each of the questions in the space below it:

1. What form did the bullying take? Who bullied you?

2. In what ways did your performance lower as a result of being bullied?

3. How did your line manager handle your lowered performance?

4. How did you handle the meeting, and to what extent did that strategy prove effective for you?

5. Looking back on it now, what could you have said or done at the meeting with your manager that could have created more effective outcomes for you?

Next Chapter

Chapter 7 focuses on the issues involved when a workplace bully targets their manager or supervisor in a campaign of upwards bullying.

Chapter 7
Bullying Upwards

Authority Issues, Anger and Passive Aggression

An Unspoken Code of Conduct

In any organisation there needs to be an unspoken code of conduct to which employees adhere if the organisation is to function effectively. This unwritten code includes deferring to the opinion of those who have greater influence, knowledge or experience than you, disagreeing constructively with senior figures when you want to challenge them, and being prepared to follow instructions issued by managers or supervisors when there are urgent issues to address. You will most likely recognise these dynamics at play in your organisation where, in the main, most employees are likely to follow them. But what happens when a member of an organisation is not willing to follow these unwritten rules of conduct, and targets either their manager or their supervisor in a campaign of workplace bullying?

This chapter explores the issues which arise when a team manager is targeted by a bullying member of their team. Although the chapter is written to 'you, the manager', it is also directly relevant to you if you have specific responsibility for supervising the work of a colleague, whether or not you have the formal title of supervisor. In this case, you find that your colleague objects to your supervision and bullies you.

In addition, the themes in the chapter may also be relevant to you even if you are not a supervisor or a manager. You may recognise the dynamics described here in your work with people who have less authority, less experience and less influence than you, and whose behaviour is aggressive and unreasonable.

A Bully in the Team

If your work involves managing other people, you will recognise that your role carries with it a level of organisational authority. Your job involves setting direction for your team members, getting the best out of each of them, and being available to them as and when they turn to you for guidance, support or direction. You expect your team members to comply with your even-handed wishes, to take on board your reasonable directives, and to work constructively with your sensible plans and proposals. For the most part, you and your team members find ways to work together effectively. Among the people in your team, there are likely to be those who have similar values to you and those who have quite different values to you. There are people you'd be comfortable chatting with on an informal basis, some with whom you don't gel, and others who have different ambitions and styles of working to yours. Nonetheless, you are paid to work effectively together for the good of your employer and, in the main, this is what happens.

Here and there, you may have disagreements with some of your team members, perhaps about specific goals or work processes. Every now and then you may have disputes with certain team members, perhaps about what information is factual and what is not, or what degree of importance each of you attaches to particular facts. Sometimes, your opinion about the values that underpin the work may diverge from that of some of the team members you manage. But, by and large, these occurrences are handled between you. You discuss the issues. You listen to one another. You resolve the differences between you and, where you can't settle them, your colleagues accept your direction. You all move on, and you don't fall out.

But, it is more complicated when one of the people in your team is a workplace bully, and decides to target you, their manager. In this situation, your team member doesn't simply disagree with you. They bully you. They disrespect your handling of your role and your authority in the organisation. Despite the fact that they report directly to you, your team member bullies you either consistently or intermittently.

The chapter examines the dynamics involved when a member of a team bullies upwards and targets their manager or supervisor in their campaign. It explores the mind-set of a bullying team member, one who is oppositional towards authority, and examines the issues involved in handling incidents of upwards bullying. It highlights the role that authority issues play in situations where a team member bullies their manager, and illustrates how active aggression or passive aggression can play a part in the dynamics of the bullying. The chapter identifies effective strategies for the manager or supervisor to use when faced with a bullying team member. It highlights strategies which a manager can use to retain control of interactions with a bullying team member, confront their bullying behaviour and re-establish their authority.

Unresolved Authority Issues

Consider the following short examples:

- A driver in a delivery firm has authority issues and bullies his manager. Every morning, at a short meeting between them in his office, the manager hands the driver a sheet of paper describing his delivery route for the day. Every morning the same bullying scene plays out between them. The driver starts by making disparaging comments about the way his manager has set out the route. He complains bitterly about the amount of work his manager has allocated to him, and attacks the 'ludicrous number of drop offs' his manager expects of him. The driver then proceeds to rage at his manager, complaining about the lack of maintenance on his van, putting forward the view that his manager is creating a 'death trap' for him, and telling him that he is a 'bastard' to work for. His face is contorted with fury as he says these things. His fists are balled and his eyes glaze over in anger. His manager lets him rage and then tells him in a quiet, strained voice that he is not responsible for the routes because they are created by computer programme. He places the sheet with the route on it on the table and leaves his office, white-faced and shaking at having been shouted at by his ranting team member.

- A team leader in the risk management department of an insurance firm bullies his manager. The team leader attends daily one-to-one briefings with his manager at which they are supposed to discuss the key issues for the day ahead. The team leader uses these meetings to make spiteful and acerbic remarks to his manager. He tells him he is a 'has-been' and is 'too old to cut it'. He refuses to make eye contact with his manager when he speaks to him, preferring to look out of the window or at the ceiling. He toys with his manager's feelings, doodling on his note pad when his manager asks him for input. His manager notes all of these unhelpful behaviours, leaves a short silence and simply repeats his question or comment, inviting a response from his team member. Invariably, his team leader ignores him and continues to display blatant disrespect for him. This scene continues until the manager concludes the meeting with the words: 'That is enough for today'. On leaving his manager's office, the bullying team leader returns to his desk alongside his team of six risk assessors. He tells his team that he has had 'a briefing of sorts from the old bloke' who manages them. He then proceeds to undermine his manager's reputation, skill-set and leadership to the bemused members of his team. He is relentless in his characterising of his manager as past it and incompetent, even though his manager is quite effective in his role and has twenty years' experience as a senior risk assessor.

Both of the managers in the short examples are decent people, experienced at their jobs. Neither of them wants to fight with their bullying team member, and both of them expect all of their team members to work constructively with them. When they each realise that they have one team member who doesn't want to work productively with them, they are thrown.

Let's examine the dynamics at play between these bullying team members and their managers. In each case, the bullying team member is able to abuse their manager because of a combination of:

- Their manager's inability to assert their authority at the time of the attack.

And:

- The team member's unusual level of disrespect for the leadership of their manager.

Both of these hard-working managers are thrown by the degree of disrespect for their authority and their position which is demonstrated by their bullying team members. Neither of the senior people can understand the degree of animosity which their team members express towards them, and neither of them knows quite what to do about it. Each of them has *quite a complicated relationship with their own authority.* When a member of their team is willing to take direction from them, they are able managers: they are comfortable setting direction, seeking influence and giving feedback. But in the unusual situation that a member of their team does not respect their authority, they both have a hard time doing any of these things effectively and are especially reluctant to *assert their right to manage.* Why do they back off in this way?

Each manager correctly discerns that the battleground between them and their team member *is* their authority. Neither of them is willing to exert their authority, or assert their right to lead, in case their team member reacts with even greater abuse. They feel intimidated, and are not able to draw a clear boundary around the disrespectful, abusive behaviour of their team member. They choose not to assert their authority in a well-meaning but misguided attempt to prevent escalating conflict, and the way is clear for the team member to continue to bully.

Both of these managers also make a misjudgement in their dealings with their abusive team member. They both think that the *reasons* their team member articulates when attacking them are real. While they dislike the aggression with which the 'reasons' are conveyed to them, they still take these 'reasons' seriously. They think that the 'reasons' represent the real issues behind the incidents of bullying. But this is not actually the case. Each of the bullying team members bullies solely because of the presence of unresolved authority issues in their lives. Their unresolved authority issues cloud their judgement of their managers, their manager's abilities as managers, and their manager's intentions towards them. The 'reasons' they cite are a smoke-screen generated by bullies who both possess limited self-awareness and great antipathy towards authority. The real explanation for their bullying lies in the fact that the bullies *want* to target their managers. It is their *will* that needs to be confronted, not the 'reasons' they generate. The more that their managers invest in discussing the 'reasons' with them, the more ground they lose, the easier it is for the bullying team member to keep inventing 'reasons,' and the easier is it for them to continue to bully.

> **Unresolved authority issues often play a part in upwards bullying.**

> **Managers who are successfully targeted often have a complicated relationship with their own authority.**

> **Bullying team members want to oppose their managers for emotionally derived reasons.**

Let's explore these issues further by going inside the mind of a bullying team member.

Inside the Mind of a Bullying Team Member

Team members who bully upwards often have authority issues. They oppose their manager as a matter of principle, for emotionally derived reasons, because they *dislike or fear authority*. They may like their manager as a person and be quite comfortable chatting informally with them at work. But as soon as the discussions move onto work topics and involve an attempt by their manager to manage them, they start to oppose. Their opposition towards their boss is not because they have considered the issues and happen to have formed a different view to theirs. It is because they oppose authority – any authority, including their manager's – on principle.

Not every team member with authority issues is a bully. There are many oppositional team members who struggle to work constructively with their managers, and who are awkward to manage, but they don't necessarily bully. Those who do bully upwards can be highly destructive towards their manager, towards the team dynamic and towards their own careers.

Team members who bully upwards do so because they:

- Dislike 'being told what to do'.

- Don't want to be managed or influenced by someone with more organisational authority than them.

- Want to retain some or all control, independence or autonomy over their work.

- Want to demonstrate consistent or intermittent disrespect for their manager's style of management.

The fundamental conflict a bullying team member faces is that they have accepted a position in an organisational hierarchy and necessarily have to report to someone. But, having done so, they seek to work against that person or that person's aims, avoiding their responsibility to work constructively for the good of their employer. The tension that plays out in their working relationship with their manager actually derives from issues inside their own life: their powerful antipathy towards authority.

In practice, bullying team members may intermittently or continuously show their disrespect for their manager's authority by taking advantage of opportunities to:

- Block progress on tasks or processes for which they are responsible, in the hope that their failure to complete their work on time and to standard will somehow result in trouble for their boss.

- Prevent actions from being taken by simply not attending to them, so they can put obstacles in the way of their boss's aims.

- Refuse to co-operate with their boss's wishes or instructions so that they can thwart them.

- Say 'it won't work' in response to a plan or proposal put forward by their boss and refuse to change their mind, without explaining why they are being so obstructive.

- Generate other plausible-sounding 'reasons' why certain actions cannot be taken, none of which are actually true, simply to oppose their boss.

- Disagree with all or most of their boss's verbal or written input to wear them down.

Bullying team members can become highly skilled at working against their manager by:

- Dodging the issues their boss puts to them, when confronted by them.

- Switching the conversation away from their aggression and oppositionality onto the supposed failings of their manager as a professional or as a person.

- Blaming their manager for aspects of their job which they dislike, think onerous, or view as unpleasant.

- Refusing to take on board any of the feedback given to them by their manager, even when they say they will, and continuing to use destructive behaviour towards them.

- Pointing out the 'rightness' of their point of view and the 'wrongness' of their manager's.

- Using active or passive aggression when speaking with their manager or about them.

The level of aggression which a bullying team member can display towards their manager can be fearsome. Some team members, like the driver, employ active aggression. Others, like the team leader, employ passive aggression. Let's explore the difference between the two forms of aggression by referring back to these two characters.

Bullying team members often fear or dislike authority.

Active Aggression

The delivery driver employs active aggression in his dealings with his manager. During their daily morning meeting, the driver rages at his manager. He contorts his face in fury. He balls his fists while speaking and his eyes glaze over with anger. He is overtly hostile, verbally and physically. He subjects his manager to a paranoid rant in which he suggests that his manager puts his life at risk by asking him to drive a van which is a 'death trap'. He accuses his manager of loading an unreasonable amount of work onto his shoulders. The driver refers to his manager as a 'bastard' who purposefully creates a difficult route for him to follow. Each morning the manager points out that the route is computer generated. The driver ignores this fact so he can harangue his manager again the following day.

In this example, the driver's authority issues and active aggression result in him simultaneously displaying:

- Unconcealed hatred towards his manager, which he verbalises and demonstrates physically.

- A desire to blame his manager in a series of unfounded, paranoid allegations.

- A desire to castigate and berate his manager in repeated uncontained, furious attacks.

- A failure to listen, learn or take any feedback on board.

It is no wonder that being subject to this extreme level of verbal and non-verbal aggression leaves his manager white-faced and shaking.

Passive Aggression

In the second example, the team leader displays passive aggression towards his manager. During and after their daily one-to-one meetings, he does not rant and yell. Instead, he employs indirect methods of conveying his aggression towards his manager. While in his manager's presence he:

- Makes spiteful and acerbic remarks, using a contemptuous tone to tell his manager that he is a 'has-been' and is 'too old to cut it'.

- Refuses to make eye contact with him, preferring to look out of the window or at the ceiling.

- Doodles on his note-pad when his manager asks him for input.

When the meeting ends and he leaves his manager's office, he continues his passive aggressive campaign behind his manager's back by:

- Informing his team members that he has had 'a briefing of sorts from the old bloke.'

- Making disparaging remarks about the manager's reputation, skill-set and leadership.

The team leader's anger is just as potent as the driver's, but his expression of it is quite different. His method is to disempower his manager to his face and undermine him behind his back. He wants to render him powerless in their one-to-one meetings, and employs a variety of passive aggressive strategies to achieve this aim.

His manager does find him extremely difficult to handle. The level of passive aggression to which he is subject severely reduces the manager's ability to conduct a productive meeting with his team leader. He tries but fails to secure any meaningful input from his bullying team member. When faced with silence or doodling, the manager either repeats his question or statement in the hope of getting an answer the second time around, or leaves a short silence before inviting the team leader to input. But neither of these tactics results in much engagement from the bully. The manager is ground down by the passive aggression to which he is subject, and ends each meeting in the same way. He says the words: 'That is enough for today.' This statement is exactly true: he really has had enough, and wants the team leader to leave his office.

But the team leader's campaign does not end there. He wants to discredit his manager behind his back as well as to his face. Not satisfied with wearing him down with passive resistance in their one-to-one meetings, he also wants to injure his reputation in the wider department. He employs the strategy of giving unfavourable reports of the manager to his own team of six people in an attempt to weaken his manager's influence with them. But he over-plays his hand and his plans backfire. His team members are bemused by his scorn towards the senior manager. They don't understand their team leader's anger towards him, nor do they agree with his unpleasant characterisations. Their view is that the senior risk assessor is experienced and worthy of respect. Their view of their *team leader's judgement* is adversely affected by his campaign of passive aggression towards the manager, and they continue to think well of the more senior man.

Let's explore the ins and outs of active and passive aggression more thoroughly, starting with the former.

The Strategy of Active Aggression

Many bullying team members feel the need to bully because their experience of authority figures at an earlier stage of their lives was poor. But, based on that experience of a hurtful, abusive or otherwise unsafe authority figure they conclude that *all authority figures* are corrupt. Bullying team members who resort to active aggression against their managers are often trying to protect themselves as best they can, but their strategy is deeply misguided and can cause great harm to those they target.

Examples of unsafe earlier authority figures include previous managers or workplace leaders, parents and other adult family members, teachers, headmasters or headmistresses, and community or religious leaders. Clearly, the generalisation from a hurtful or abusive experience with one or several authority figures earlier in their life, to the conclusion that every workplace authority figure will also be hurtful or corrupt, is not necessarily true. It fails to make the distinction between:

- Well-intentioned workplace authority figures who need to learn some or all of the skills of effective leadership.

And:

- Malign, ill-intentioned workplace authority figures who use their position to abuse those whom they lead.

Their earlier experience was of the latter. But they allow that experience to colour their perception in the workplace to the extent that they don't recognise the former. Instead of forming individual judgements about the merits, skills, areas for development and intentions of their manager, bullying team members take the view that *because they are a manager they must be unsafe or corrupt*. They use this often unconsciously-held belief as a pretext for aggression.

In their minds, the active aggression they employ is necessary as a:

- *Shield*: to protect themselves from the corrupt authority figure, and prevent that person from humiliating them, shaming them, or placing them in a position of vulnerability.

- *Weapon*: with which to attack the authority figure and keep them at a distance.

- *Punishment*: for a perceived insult or slight by the authority figure, or for an action taken by the authority figure to which they object.

- *Method of control*: so that they can exert some influence over the authority figure with respect to key issues or in certain situations.

- *Cover for their fear*: for example, fear of the authority figure exposing their weaknesses, lack of skills or perceived inadequacies.

The driver employs the strategy of active aggression, but his ferocious verbal and physical assault on his manager completely misses the well-intentioned manager's only motive: to do a good job.

The driver allows his uncontained rage at authority figures to cloud his judgement to the extent that he fabricates a series of serious allegations against his manager, allegations which he tells him about in a full-on volley of ranting rage. There is not on iota of truth to anything the driver says. His manager has not set up a 'death trap' for him. His van is in good working order. He has not loaded extra work onto the driver's shoulders. The amount of work allocated to the driver is consistent with the amount of work allocated to all the other drivers. He has not created an onerous route for him to travel. The route is computer generated and is the shortest, most sensible route given the deliveries he needs to make that day. The driver is in serious need of attending to the anger issues in his life. If he does not do so, he may well find that he jeopardises his employment with the delivery firm.

The Strategy of Passive Aggression

Bullying team members who resort to passive aggression are also using a highly misguided strategy. The strategy of passive aggression is often rooted in the fact that they have not developed healthy ways of talking about anger. Instead of speaking about the issues in order to resolve them, they bottle up their anger and let it out in indirect ways. They may:

- Express their anger using resistant and obstructive means when they are in the presence of the authority figure.

- Continue to express their anger by slandering and undermining the authority figure behind their back.

- Try and persuade other colleagues that the authority figure is a poor manager or is otherwise incompetent and not to be trusted.

- Ignore or refute feedback from colleagues who challenge their unfavourable view of the authority figure.

- Strain their relationships with colleagues who question their prejudiced view of the manager.

- Fail to notice the repeating pattern whereby they injure their relationships with colleagues because their prejudiced comments bring their judgement into question.

The team leader employs the strategy of passive aggression, but he is blind to the fact he is doing so. He thinks that he is justified in his view that the senior manager is too old to do his job, and ought to be removed from his post and replaced with a younger, more competent man. The problem for him is that there is no evidence to support this view.

While it is true that his boss is older than he is, it is also true that he is competent and experienced at his job. It does not occur to the team leader that his *belief about his senior manager's supposed incompetence* is completely faulty, that the senior manager is well respected and rightly so, and that the issues which need addressing are actually *in his own life*. He is so sure of his own opinion that he continues with his view even when his team members look bemused, and refuse to collude with his assessment of the senior manager. He doesn't notice that his strategy of bad-mouthing his manager to his team members is losing him their respect, goodwill and active co-operation. He continues with his campaign of passive aggression and injures his reputation with his own team. He continues to blind himself to the fact that he is in woeful need of attending to his own development issues.

What Bullying Team Members Want, and What They Need

What a bullying team member WANTS is to disrespect their manager's authority. What they NEED is to work for a manager who resolutely refuses to be disrespected, who remains fully invested in their authority, and who requires the bully to perform effectively. The bullying team member may NOT LIKE the fact that their manager asserts their right to manage them. But the bully does NEED a manager who is prepared to do this if they are to look inwards, confront themselves, and resolve their authority issues.

What a bullying team member wants to achieve is two-fold: to disrespect the authority of their manager *and* cause their manager to relinquish their authority so that the bully can acquire it. The bully is motivated to disrespect their manager's authority and demonstrates that disrespect via active or passive aggression, or both. They demonstrate their opposition both in the presence of their manager and behind their back. Often, a key goal in their campaign is to unsettle their manager sufficiently that the manager *chooses to surrender their authority to the bully in the moment of an attack*. The bully wants to *disempower* their manager, and acquire their authority for themselves.

Faced with these dynamics, many managers may make the well-intentioned mistake of relinquishing their authority in an attempt to placate the bully. But this strategy will not result in them being subject to a lower level of aggression – in fact, it encourages the bully.

To handle each attack effectively, keep in mind that what the bully WANTS and NEEDS are quite different. Managers need to retain their authority in each and every meeting with the bully, and use it to confront the bullying. As a manager you could do this by:

- Recognising that you are having a hard time asserting your authority when in the presence of the bully.

- Confronting the fact that by not using your full authority you are, however unwittingly, making it easy for the bully to bully.

- Recognising that while it is true that the bully does not respect your authority and wants to oppose it, you need to assert your right to manage them in every encounter you have with them.

- Challenging oppositional behaviour whenever you are subject to it, using a resolute, factual and unemotional tone.

Bullying team members NEED to work for a manager who is unafraid to assert their authority, even though they may not WANT this.

Let's return to the two short examples and apply these principles. We will begin by outlining the options available to the delivery company manager.

Asserting Your Authority

The delivery company manager is appalled at the level of aggression directed at him by the driver. He is so shocked at the repeated attacks on him that he becomes paralysed and uses the same ineffective behaviour in the daily briefing with the delivery driver. He is unable to protect himself against the driver's rage in any of these meetings. Each morning, he waits in his office for the driver to arrive, hands the delivery sheet to him, endures the abusive rage of his driver, and reminds him that the delivery route is computer generated. He then leaves his office. He hopes that the level of aggression his driver generates each day will abate at some point, and that perhaps that day's encounter will be less abusive. He waits passively for the bully to cease using bullying behaviour. His strategy does not achieve the outcomes he desires: for the bully to cease bullying him. Of course the driver hears the words he says every day – that the route is computer generated - but he ignores them so he can bully his manager the following day on the same pretext.

The delivery company manager would better serve his own cause by stepping back from the incidents, taking a deep breath and asserting his right to manage the driver in the moment of the attack. To achieve this he could use:

- *His body language*: he needs to use a clear, firm and unswerving tone, and maintain level eye contact with his bullying team member throughout each meeting. He needs to keep his shoulders back, and his head held high.

- *His resolve*: he needs to see the aggression for what it is – a crude tactic – and refuse to be thrown by it. He needs to assert his authority in his own office.

- *His status:* he needs to keep clearly in mind that he is the manager and use his organisational status to his advantage.

Here are a couple of ways he could handle the situation:

- As soon as his driver enters the room he needs to be on the front foot, delivery sheet in hand, and walk smartly towards him. He needs to seize the momentum straight away and say: 'Here is your computer-generated delivery route for today.' He could hand the sheet to the driver or place it on the desk, and simply walk out of the office, leaving the driver standing by himself. The manager does not have to remain in his office and allow himself to be subject to aggression.

- The manager knows that none of the paranoid accusations yelled by the driver are true. So, he could wait in his office for the attack to begin, and write down the paranoid accusations in full view of the driver, contemporaneous with the assault. Then, again with the driver's knowledge, he could make a photocopy of the handwritten notes, and give it to the driver. He could tell him to go away, read over what he said and return to that office at the end of the day to discuss the issues with him. The clear implication of this strategy is that firstly, the manager is in charge not the driver, and secondly, that the driver has some explaining to do. Put like this, the driver will probably avoid the meeting at the end of the day. He may remain sullen and difficult to handle in future encounters with the manager, but he is unlikely to abuse him again. However, should the driver continue with his campaign against the manager, and claim that the manager has made up the words he attributes to him on the sheet, then the manager can counter by saying that there will be a witness in his office the following morning for the briefing between the two of them. The presence of the witness – another colleague – will make it highly likely that the bullying behaviour will stop.

The senior risk assessor also has choices available to him, as a manager, which he is not utilising. To challenge the passive aggression of the team leader he needs to:

- Play back to the bullying team leader the behaviour which he finds so disrespectful.

- Require him to participate actively and constructively in the meeting.

The manager's best interests will be well served by holding up a mirror to the team leader so that the younger man can see how he is coming across. Although the team leader's disrespect is aimed at the manager, the manager's task is to enable the team leader to *confront himself*. Each time the team leader uses a rude, disrespectful, passive aggressive behaviour the manager needs to verbalise it in clear, factual terms and play it straight back to the team member.

There are a number of ways in which the manager could do this, each of which achieves a slightly different outcome for him. Let's explore three of them.

- In a calm and non-accusatory, descriptive tone the manager could say: 'I asked you a question just now to which you have not responded. I can see that you are doodling on the page in front of you. You are not making eye contact with me. What do you mean by this behaviour?' Uttered in a neutral and calm tone, these words will be highly confrontational for the team leader. They require that he explain himself and engage with the substance of the meeting, rather than use his energy to resist his manager. They require that he attend to the business issues he is paid to discuss with his manager, rather than allow himself to be driven by his inner anger. Being called to account in this clear, factual and non-aggressive way by his manager requires him to use different behaviour in the meeting.

- Alternatively, in a clear and confident tone, the manager could say: 'I asked you a question just now to which you have not responded. Let me be quite clear. I want you to participate constructively in this meeting or come back later when you are ready to do so.' This more direct confrontation re-establishes the manager's authority in his own office, asserts his right to expect a level of input from his team leader, and makes it clear that he is not satisfied with his team leader's performance. It challenges the team leader to return to his manager's office when he is ready to work effectively. However, should the team leader respond to this challenge with insolence, perhaps by remaining motionless and silent in his chair, the manager could get up, open his office door leaving it wide open, and return to his seat. He could then say: 'I am serious. I want you to participate constructively in this meeting or come back later when you are ready to do so. The door is open. Which is it to be?'

- The third option available to the manager is to adopt a neutral and unemotional tone and say: 'I asked you a question just now to which you have not responded. This is another example of the disrespect you have shown towards me recently. You can continue to disrespect me, in which case I will continue to challenge you. Or you can stop disrespecting me. Which is it to be?' This response from the manager is powerful and influential. His team leader now has a choice: continue to be rude and disrespectful and face the consequences, or cease being rude and disrespectful and participate constructively. Either way he will find it difficult to continue with his campaign of passive aggression.

All of these approaches retain control for the manager. All of them preserve his personal power and enable him to use his organisational authority to demand a suitable level of engagement from his team member. Crucially, all of these options require that the team leader ceases using passive aggression, and takes an active role in the meeting even if it is only to leave the room.

Each of these approaches is powerful and influential because each of them provides the team leader with what he NEEDS - clear, decisive and non-abusive leadership - while preventing him from having what he WANTS - control of the room. This combination of factors challenges the team member's fundamental assumption that all authority is abusive, incompetent or otherwise unsafe. He will learn that his manager is not intimidated by his passive aggression, is quite able to draw the line and can hold him to account. He will learn that his manager:

- Respects his own position and the authority that goes with it.

- Does not misuse that authority, or act abusively towards him, even when under considerable pressure.

- Wants him to perform effectively, and contribute more to the meeting than he is currently doing.

None of these options will necessarily prevent the team leader from leaving the room and bad-mouthing his manager to his own team members, but they will all put him on the back foot the *next time* he enters his manager's office. The team leader will be anxious: he will not know what to expect. He will know that the last time he was in his manager's office the tables turned, and his manager got the better of him. It is important that, having drawn the line effectively by asserting his authority, that the manager continue to do so in each and every subsequent meeting with his team leader. He cannot afford to relax – he needs to maintain his authoritative and assertive demeanour whenever he is working in the same room as the team leader.

How the team leader handles his issues from the moment of being called to account by his manager will be a clear test of his character. His challenge is to:

- Confront his development issues.

- Cease acting out his anger towards his manager.

- Stop bad-mouthing his manager behind his back.

- Reverse the trend of losing the respect of his team members.

If the team leader is unable to do any of these things, he is likely to continue to create dynamics in his working relationships which work against his best interests, while continuing to blind himself to the fact that it is *he, himself* - and not his manager – who has development issues.

> **Your body language, your will and your resolve are key tools for asserting your authority.**

> **Describe the behaviour you observe in a non-evaluative tone and ask: 'what do you mean by this behaviour?'**

> **Present your team member with a clear choice: participate constructively or come back later.**

> **Present your team member with a clear choice: continue to disrespect you and be challenged, or cease being disrespectful.**

Both of the above short examples concern interactions between well-intentioned, able managers and their bullying team members. Let's explore the issues involved in a more complicated scenario, one in which a supervisor has areas for development and is not effective in his role, and in which a bullying team member uses both active and passive aggression.

Case Study 5: Lies and Innuendo

A small team in a local council is run by an ineffective supervisor. The supervisor is a lazy man who doesn't like his job. He experiences the quiet and studious atmosphere of the council as stifling, and doesn't leave his office very often. A solitary figure, he thinks that working for a local council is a dull way to spend his days, but doesn't look for another job. He doesn't apply himself to the detail of his work and is regularly late for team meetings, but expects his team members to produce work that is accurate and timely. His small team of four people sits in an open plan area outside his office. They are regularly irritated by his double standards and quietly complain about him behind his back, but work well together.

An administrator is asked to move into the supervisor's team from her role in another team in the council. She does not want to do so and says she would prefer to stay where she is, working for a man she gets on well with. She says that she enjoys a positive working relationship with her current supervisor, and that she has performed well under his tutelage. She is told that, under a re-structuring plan, the duties which she performs will become part of the supervisor's responsibilities, and she must report to him. She joins his team with a heavy heart.

Her first meeting with the supervisor does not go well. She notes his downcast appearance, the way he slouches behind his desk, and the fact that he appears distracted during the meeting. She notes that his gaze drifts towards the window while she is speaking to him and feels offended by his lack of eye contact. Towards the end of the meeting she snaps at him: 'Are you listening to me?' to which he replies in an irritated and angry manner: 'Of course I am!' But his manner towards her does not alter throughout the remainder of the meeting, and she leaves feeling offended.

Their subsequent meetings continue in much the same vein. The supervisor does an adequate job of managing her, but no more than this. The administrator becomes visibly more fed up at her manager's apparent lack of interest in her work. Three weeks into her new role, the administrator snaps. She leaves the supervisor's office and returns to her own desk. By the time she is seated, she is visibly shaking. Unable to contain her anger at being treated as unimportant by her new supervisor, she embarks on a campaign of workplace bullying, targeting him.

Initially, she speaks unkindly about him behind his back, parodying him as a hapless fool who is lucky to be in a job. Over the next few days, she tells everyone in the team, and anyone outside of it who will listen, that he is an inept supervisor who is out of his depth. She says that she and her fellow team members would be 'better off by ourselves.' One morning she shares a lift with the supervisor's manager. She takes advantage of this coincidence by telling the manager that 'the supervisor's bungling is jeopardising the work of the team'.

After two weeks of bad-mouthing him behind his back, she escalates her campaign to include attacking him in his office. As she is about to leave his office after their Friday one-to-one meeting, she asks him if he is 'aware what the people out there are saying?' She drops this question nonchalantly onto the table and watches to see how the supervisor reacts. She is annoyed by his apparent indifference to the suggestion that he is the subject of tittle tattle, so she ups the ante. In an openly sarcastic tone she says: 'I'd be mortified to hear that kind of stuff said about me!' Again, she watches his face to gauge his reaction. She forms the view that the supervisor is insufficiently unsettled by her strategy of suggesting that his team members and colleagues are gossiping about him. So, at their meeting on the following Monday, and at every subsequent meeting, she makes disparaging remarks about his appearance, his manner and his supervision of the team, using a cutting and demeaning tone. On each occasion, the supervisor appears outwardly unmoved, apparently wishing to give the impression that he is unperturbed by his new team member's aggression. After a fortnight of subjecting him to daily insults and humiliating comments, the administrator makes a further more clinical assault on him in a planned escalation of her campaign.

She begins her next one-to-one meeting with him by telling the supervisor that he is 'failing the team' and 'letting everyone down', generalisations which she utters in a contemptuous and belittling tone. This time the supervisor appears shocked at her venomous tone. He remains still and silent behind his desk, waiting to see what she will say next. The administrator stands up in front of him and announces that his incompetence makes her angry and she doesn't want to be angry. She shouts over him when he briefly tries to defend himself, telling him in withering tones that he shows an appalling lack of judgement and a level of ineptitude that is staggering. In the silence that follows she sits down again. In a quiet and measured tone, she tells the supervisor that no one has any faith in him anymore and that they think they are wasting their time working for him. Encouraged by his frozen expression, she proceeds to tell him that he is so poor at his job, and his reputation is so tattered, that he would be better off running his decisions past her so she can make sure he handles things properly and doesn't get into any more hot water. She ends by saying that she would ask him to apologise to her for being so weak and ineffectual a supervisor, but she realises that someone who is as poor as him at nurturing talent and rewarding effort would not understand what she is talking about.

She pauses for a moment, smiles at him with head on one side, and says: 'I'd better get on with my work now, and save you from getting anything else wrong today.' She walks smartly out of his office, leaving the supervisor spiralling into self-doubt as he considers the possibility that most of his team members are gossiping about him, are laughing at him behind his back, and think he is a terrible person to work for.

Analysing the Dynamics in Case Study 5: Lies and Innuendo

In this case study, an unimpressive supervisor is subject to workplace bullying by his new team member. He is an easy target for her campaign of lies and innuendo due to his habit of spending a lot of time by himself in his office, his solitariness, and his shoddy approach to his work. He is an adequate supervisor at best, uninterested in his team members or their work, and a poor role-model.

The administrator is a complicated character who had a positive relationship with her previous supervisor, a man with whom she got on well. There was no hint of her vicious aggression in her dealings with him. But, almost as soon as she has her first meeting with the supervisor, she takes against him and the scene is set for her escalating campaign of workplace bullying. What are the factors in her life which create the impetus to bully?

Need for Approval

The administrator's complex character is rooted in the fact that she *craves approval from an authority figure at work.* As long as she receives sufficient approval from her supervisor she remains a hardworking, constructive member of the team. She thrives under her previous supervisor from whom she received both genuine praise and consistent endorsement. This combination of attention and approval results in her latent aggression towards authority remaining dormant. But as soon as she starts to work for the new supervisor, things take a different turn.

The administrator approaches her first meeting with the supervisor as openly as she can. She has heard reports about the distant and unsupportive style of her new supervisor. Nonetheless, she is not prepared for quite how detached and uninterested he is. During their first meeting, the supervisor appears obviously indifferent to her presence, doesn't listen to her, and even looks out of the window while she is speaking to him.

Towards the end of the meeting she snaps at him: 'Are you listening to me?' in the hope that he will realise that his behaviour is unacceptable and change his demeanour towards her. But she is disappointed. Her rebuke does not cause him to change his manner at all. Instead, he retorts: 'Of course I am!' in an irritated and angry tone, and continues to behave in the same blasé and unresponsive manner. These actions signal to the administrator that her new supervisor is bored in her presence, is not willing to give her his attention or the level of approval she needs, and is unlikely to be open to her influence. She misinterprets his complacency and lack of interest in his job as *active disapproval of her*. This is an intolerable conclusion for the administrator to arrive at. She cannot bear the thought of being disapproved of by her supervisor, and her latent authority issues crystalize into action. She decides to take revenge for his lack of approval of her by bullying the supervisor.

Calculated Attack

Having made the decision to bully her supervisor, the administrator is ruthless in her execution of her plan. Her campaign consists of a number of inter-connected phases, each of which involves an increasing level of aggression.

- Initially, she uses *passive aggression to parody the supervisor* to anyone who will listen. She characterises him behind his back as a hapless and inept fool. She tells her new team members that they would be better off without him. She extends her campaign of parodying him to include the supervisor's manager. In a chance meeting with the manager in a lift, the administrator describes the supervisor's leadership of the team as 'bungling' and claims he is jeopardising the work of the team.

- Having prepared the ground behind his back, the administrator then *employs active aggression to his face.* She asks him if he is aware what people around the office are saying about him. When he appears unperturbed by the suggestion that unkind things are being said about him, the administrator ups the ante. She says that she would be mortified to be subject to the kind of comments regularly being made about the supervisor. This is a disingenuous thing to do as it conceals the truth that she is the person who is slandering him amid the suggestion that it is the actions of people other than herself which he ought to be concerned about. However, when this level of innuendo fails to puncture him, she decides to employ a greater level of direct aggression.

- In her subsequent meetings with him, *she attacks the supervisor in a series of humiliating rebukes.* She makes disparaging remarks about his appearance, his demeanour and his supervision of the team. After a fortnight of subjecting him to daily insults and humiliating comments, she notes that he does not do anything to defend himself at the time of her attacks. She devises a ferocious assault on him.

- Her plan involves *a display of overt, cunning aggression.* She tells the supervisor that he is failing everyone in the team and letting them down. This is a calculated move because it is *she herself* not 'people out there' who are bad-mouthing him. Although his team members grumble about him, they do not castigate and berate him behind his back like she does. The administrator says this to mislead the supervisor about who his real adversary is, while simultaneously portraying herself as a concerned team member who wants to warn him about the reputational damage he is incurring around the office. Neither of the claims she makes is true. The supervisor is not an effective supervisor, but he is not letting everyone down or failing them. Both of these claims are lies devised by the administrator to cause the supervisor to doubt himself. She wants him to think that everyone thinks ill of him. She wants him to feel isolated, confused and disoriented. *She says these things in an attempt to disempower the supervisor.* In a display of open aggression, she then stands up and shouts at him, blaming him for her anger, and portraying him as witheringly incompetent. At this point the supervisor is in shock. He has a frozen expression on his face, and he is immobile. The administrator thinks she is, at last, getting somewhere. So, *she tries to acquire his authority for herself* by telling him in a quiet and measured tone that no one has any faith in him anymore, that his reputation is torn to shreds, and that he needs to run his decisions past her in future if he is avoid getting into any further hot water. These are very unkind things to say to someone who has done her no actual harm. They are also completely untrue. The other team members do quietly complain about the supervisor, and resent his double standards. But no one has lost complete faith in him. Lastly, *she makes a second attempt to usurp his authority* by suggesting that the supervisor owes her an apology. She tells him that he is a weak and ineffectual supervisor, and that she realises it would be pointless asking for an apology from someone as poor as he is at nurturing talent and rewarding effort. She walks out of his office suggesting that without her to aid him, the day's work would be a disaster, so she had better go and attend to her duties. These are very telling words indeed. The administrator presents herself as someone whose talent and effort have gone unrewarded, and whose endeavour alone is preventing catastrophe from overwhelming the supervisor. None of these comments are true, but they are very revealing. They illustrate how she is feeling: under-valued, under-recognised and disregarded by her manager. They also reveal the nature of her true hatred for the supervisor.

The administrator's strategy involves lying about her supervisor around the office, before lying to him in a series of increasingly devious and slanderous falsehoods. Since he is a solitary figure in the council offices, someone who doesn't seek the company of colleagues and doesn't leave his office very much, she hopes that he will believe some or all of her lies and innuendos, and feel crushed. Let's take a look at this series of incidents through his eyes. We will start by assessing his character before identifying a series of strategies he could use to:

- Assert his authority in his own office.

- Manage the administrator's behaviour at the time of the attacks.

- Require her to participate constructively in her meetings with him.

Double Standards

The supervisor is a complacent and irresponsible man who fails to apply himself effectively to his job. He somehow squares performing less-than-adequately with his conscience, and overlooks his own double standards. He consistently asks more of his staff than of himself, and is genuinely displeased to have another team member to supervise. He doesn't want the extra responsibility or the work involved in supervising an additional person, and can't be bothered to speak with her properly during their first meeting. He goes through the motions of this meeting, but his mind is elsewhere. His off-hand and disinterested manner understandably annoys the administrator and she snaps at him: 'Are you listening to me?' Instead of taking responsibility for the fact that he has not been listening, has been looking out of the window, and isn't concentrating, he simply says: 'Of course I am!' in a visibly irritated manner.

The supervisor misses the importance of this crucial moment. Had he taken the rebuke seriously, decided to give his attention to the administrator, and done his job competently, it is probable that he would have avoided the onslaught of passive aggression, rage and authority issues to which he was subsequently subject. This in no way removes responsibility from the administrator for devising such a vicious form of revenge, but it does represent a clear missed opportunity for the supervisor to act in his own – and his employer's - best interests. Instead, he mishandles the moment, fails to take the administrator's reasonable question on board, and continues to display open disinterest for her work during their subsequent meetings. He becomes subject to a cunning and calculated campaign of workplace bullying.

Resisting Falsehood and Slander

Let's look at how the supervisor could handle each of the phases of the campaign effectively. We will take the phases in order, highlighting strategies the supervisor could employ to combat false accusation, slander and innuendo.

- The first stage of the administrator's campaign is conducted behind the supervisor's back when she characterises him as an inept fool. At this point, it is quite hard for him to defend himself because he is not present when she says these things. Indeed, because he spends so much time in his office by himself and does not venture much outside it, he may be completely unaware that anything untoward is being said about him. He only becomes aware of the comments being perpetrated against him when the administrator tells him that she'd be mortified if she was subject to the kinds of remarks being made about him.

As soon as he hears these words, and even though he does not know what is being said or that she is the one doing the slandering, the supervisor needs to cease being passive and uninvolved, and become active and alert. He needs to say: 'What does that mean?' This may be quite a challenging thing for him to say because he may not want to know what is being said. But he needs to put the administrator on the spot and require her to be open. He needs to challenge her to stop using fuzzy, generalised innuendo and speak plainly. The administrator will find this question quite hard to handle. She knows full well that it is she herself who is slandering and parodying the supervisor, not any of her colleagues. She will be on the back foot, and explaining what she means by her remark will not be a straightforward thing for her to do. Planning what lies and slanders to articulate in advance is one thing. Inventing falsehood on the spur of the moment as a cover for previous falsehood is quite another. In and of itself, it is unlikely that the question 'What does that mean?' will result in the administrator halting her campaign against the supervisor. But she will realise that the supervisor is not the soft target she assessed him to be, and this knowledge will give her pause for thought.

- The next opportunity for the supervisor to redress the balance between them occurs when the administrator verbalises a series of unkind opinions to him, over the period of a fortnight, presenting each one as a fact. Every time she articulates an insult, the supervisor needs to challenge it. He could let her complete her insulting comment before saying. 'That may or may not be true, but I am still your supervisor,' before steering the conversation back to the work they are there to discuss. If she is unwilling to take this hint, he could respond more directly and say: 'Another insulting remark? You are on a roll today. Let's get back to work.' Each of these retorts achieves a slightly different result for him. The first makes it quite clear that he does not automatically buy into her version of events. It tells her that she can relay information to him if she wants to, but he will decide for himself what is true and what is not, *and* remain her supervisor, fully in charge of the meeting. The second retort neatly deflects her rudeness, making a wry joke out of her attempt to unsettle him. It tells her that she has failed to ruffle him, that he alone is in charge of how he feels, and he expects their dialogue to focus on the work they are there to discuss.

- The next opportunity for the supervisor to assert his authority occurs when the administrator tells him that he is 'failing the team' and 'letting everyone down'. Again, the supervisor needs to find out what she means. Leaning back comfortably in his chair, using a clear and straightforward tone, he could say: 'So, you want me to believe that I am failing the team and letting everyone down?' This retort takes the point of the attack away from her insult and re-focuses it around *her*. It plays her words straight back to her and places the energy of the meeting back on her. Now she has to find something to say, something which expands on and explains her previous remark. This is a clever response for the supervisor to give because he does not know whether she is telling him the truth or not. This response enables him to test the waters and see how she replies. If her feedback is genuine, and there is substance to what she is saying, her next comments will demonstrate her sincerity and explain her concerns. But, since her comments are not sincere but are fabrications, she will be hard pressed to back them up with anything concrete because she is the only person who feels like that.

- The next opportunity for the supervisor to challenge the bully is when she claims that he is making her angry and blames him for her feelings. He needs to pounce on this. He could look her firmly in the eye and say: 'I am not responsible for your aggression. You are.' Or he could say: 'You generate your aggression all by yourself. I don't have anything to do with it.' Either of these retorts draws a clear boundary around her anger, and requires the administrator to take responsibility for generating her own emotion.

- Next, when the administrator tells him that no one has any faith in him and they all think they are wasting their time working for him, the supervisor needs to act. He could say: 'You think that everyone in this office has lost faith in me. So you said. I heard you. It's your opinion.' This response tells her that she can say what she wants to say as often as she wants to say it, but that he considers what she says to be simply an opinion, not a fact. It tells her that her tactic of verbally lashing him is not unsettling him, does not frighten him, and is actually quite impotent because he and he alone decides what is fact and what is not. Since much of what the administrator says to the supervisor is her opinion dressed up as a fact, this represents a powerful way of disarming her.

- Finally, when the administrator tells the supervisor that he owes her an apology but that she isn't going to ask for one from someone as incompetent as he is, the supervisor needs to go straight back at her. He could say: 'From where I am sitting, there are some pluses to having you on the team. You do a good job most of the time. Your work is, in the main, accurate and on time. But, there are plenty of minuses to having you around as well. These include the level of aggression and intimidation you feel it necessary to use in your dealings with me, your desire to undermine me, and your suggestion that I need to apologise to you.' This is a powerful response for the supervisor to make. It is clear, factual and arresting. It simultaneously asserts his right, as the administrator's supervisor, to evaluate her performance while also critiquing her conduct in unimpeachably fair terms. It gives the administrator little or no room for manoeuvre and makes it quite clear where the true organisational authority lies in the meeting - with the supervisor.

Given the depth of the administrator's anger towards him, it is likely that the supervisor will need to challenge her over and over again before she relents. If he doesn't do this – if he continues to allow the administrator to come into his office and bully him occasionally or consistently – his self-esteem will become compromised and he may end up in a precarious position with his employer. He is not influential or well known in the council. His work is under-par. He has a reputation as an employee with a lackadaisical approach to his duties. These factors will not work in his favour should his performance become even more compromised as a result of being bullied.

However, the challenge facing the supervisor extends beyond his need to confront his bullying team member. It includes a clear need for him to take responsibility for consistently under-performing, for setting a poor example as a supervisor, and for allowing these issues to go unaddressed for a long time. He has much work to do if he is to become an asset to his employer and an effective supervisor to his team members.

> **When confronted with unclear innuendo, say: 'what does that mean?'**

> **To deflect an insult say: 'that may or may not be true, but I am still your supervisor'.**

> **Play the oppositional bully's words straight back to them in the form of a question: "so, you want me to believe that I am failing the team and letting everyone down?"**

> **Clarify that you alone decide what represents an opinion, and what represents a fact.**

> **Outline the pluses and minuses to having the bully on your team, being fair in your assessment of their strengths and weaknesses.**

Resolving Authority Issues

Let's now return to the administrator and examine the impact of a series of effective challenges by the supervisor on her relationship with him, and on her authority issues. The administrator's underlying issue is that she fears disapproval from an authority figure and as a result of this, she misinterprets the supervisor's shoddy approach to his work. She wrongly concludes that his apparent lack of interest in the meeting with her is evidence of his active disapproval of her. She bullies him in revenge for his perceived lack of approval of her. Her campaign involves undermining his reputation around the office and attacking him to his face. She wants to injure his self-esteem and cause him to doubt himself so much that he relinquishes his authority to her.

By challenging her bullying of him using a non-evaluative, non-aggressive but confident tone, while simultaneously asserting his right to supervise her, the supervisor tells the administrator that he:

- Is unafraid of exerting his authority.

- Knows how to retain it under pressure.

- Knows how to use it in a non-destructive and calm manner to clarify that *she reports to him.*

- Expects her to handle herself in a constructive way while in a meeting with him.

- Is quite willing to work with her, albeit she needs to cease being abusive and participate positively in the meeting.

By sending her these messages, the supervisor challenges the administrator's view that he is an authority figure who disapproves of her. Instead, he requires her to confront the fact that, not only is he willing to work with her, he is willing to work with her despite the fact that she is being abusive: hardly the actions of a judgemental and critical supervisor. It will take considerable resolve for the supervisor to handle the administrator effectively. But, as he continues to assert his authority over her in a calm and non-evaluative way, so it becomes more difficult for the administrator to continue to *undermine his relationship with his authority*. Eventually, she will have to desist, a situation which sets up the possibility that the administrator will decide to look inwards and address the real issues in her working life: her once latent, but now active, authority issues.

However, there is always the possibility that the administrator does not look inwards, but continues to find working for the supervisor intolerable. In this case, the administrator has choices. She could:

- Make the best of it and continue to work as part of the supervisor's team.

- Look for another job in the council or with another employer.

If she decides to continue to work in the supervisor's team, she could use the organisational 360 feedback processes to provide constructive feedback on his performance. Equally, if she decides to leave and work elsewhere, she could give her feedback during an exit interview. In either case, she doesn't have to dilute the feedback. She can tell it like it is, starting with her dissatisfaction with the supervisor's conduct in the first meeting between the two of them. But she needs to make the decision to provide constructive feedback as part of a strategy which is aimed at improving the work standards of the team and the performance of her supervisor. She must not allow her unresolved - and previously latent - authority issues to become an excuse for a campaign of workplace bullying.

Summary of Key Points from the Chapter

Many team members who bully upwards do so because they have unresolved authority issues. They fear or dislike you, their manager or supervisor, on principle and for emotionally derived reasons. Your bullying team member is motivated to oppose you, your aims or your authority, not because they have thought about the issues and happen to arrive at a different view to yours. They oppose you because they want to.

Some bullying team members need approval from their manager, a workplace authority figure, and resort to bullying methods when they think – rightly or wrongly – that you don't approve of them.

A bullying team member may employ direct, active aggression. In this case, their open displays of anger towards you can be quite overwhelming. Alternatively, a bullying team member may employ indirect, passive aggression towards you. In this case, they resist you to your face and continue their campaign against you behind your back. Sometimes, the degree of rage they subject you to can be simply astonishing in its persistence and venom.

A bullying team member probably opposes authority in a misguided attempt to protect themselves. They are likely to hold the unconscious belief that all authority is incompetent, corrupt or otherwise unsafe. They allow this view to colour their perception of you and your management style, and to influence their behaviour towards you. They are likely to make your authority the battleground between the two of you but, actually, the real issue they are struggling with lies within their own life. Their true need is to safely process the unresolved anger they feel from their past experiences of unsafe or abusive authority figures, so that they can interact with you and other current workplace authority figures from a clean space.

Although you may be tempted to give in and relinquish your authority to the bully in order to keep the peace, this is a counter-productive tack to take. While a bullying team member may WANT to oppose your authority and remove power from you, what they NEED is for you to hold the boundary as their authority figure. It is important that you continue to assert your right to manage the bully, especially in the moment of an attack, and don't fall into the trap of surrendering your authority to them during these encounters.

Their disrespect for you and your authority will not burn itself out over time. It needs to be confronted. You need to confront the bully, using a calm and non-evaluative manner, every time they employ an actively aggressive or a passively aggressive tactic. The most effective way to do this is to continue to manage the bullying team member by giving them feedback, requiring them to perform to standard, challenging their abusive words, confronting their active aggression, and inviting them to use open and transparent behaviour instead of passive aggression.

Your overall aim is to challenge the bully, repeatedly if necessary, until they re-evaluate their prejudiced view that your expression of authority is dangerous or worthy of contempt, realise that it is they who have a pressing need to address their development needs, and choose to respect your authority.

Questions for You to Consider

You may now like to apply the material from this chapter to your own working life. Bring to mind a specific situation in which you observed a team member bullying upwards, or in which you were targeted by one of your team members. You can jot down your answers to each of the following questions in the space below it:

1. Who bullied whom? In what situations did they bully?

2. What tactics did the bully employ? How did the target (or you) respond at the time?

3. How successful was the target (or you) at asserting their authority in the moment of an attack?

4. Looking back on it now, what could the target (or you) have said or done differently that would have been more effective at confronting the bullying and asserting their (or your) authority?

Next Chapter

Chapter 8 focuses on the issues facing non-bullying team members who recognise that their team leader is being targeted by a team colleague, and want to know how to make a positive contribution to the situation.

Chapter 8
Bullying in Your Team Meeting

Responding Effectively When Your Manager
Is the Target

Observing Bullying in Your Team Meeting

If you think that a workplace bully may be targeting your manager or supervisor at a team meeting, you will know just how difficult it can be to intervene effectively. Do you say something to the bully and risk becoming their next target? Do you remain silent and become a passive enabler of the bullying? The challenge is all the more tricky to address if your team manager doesn't know how to handle the bullying effectively. Maybe your manager tries to placate the bully. Or maybe they fail see the bullying for what it is, and engage in fruitless, time-consuming discussions about the merits of the various 'reasons' the bully puts forward. Perhaps the bully dominates your team meetings, taking them away from the business you are there to discuss onto their favourite topics or gripes. You, along with other members of your team, respect your manager and want to intervene on their behalf. But you don't know how to do so effectively, and feel powerless to prevent further attacks.

If you have experience of saying something to the bully in the meeting, perhaps by pointing out how unreasonable or aggressive they are being, you may find that instead of moderating their behaviour, the bully simply speaks over you, ignores you or puts you down, and carries on in the same vein. Others of you may opt to keep quiet at the time of the attack, but have a word with the bully after the meeting. However, suggesting to the bully that they tone down their language or behaviour might not prove straightforward. Instead of taking your feedback on board, the bully displays considerable agility at avoiding it. They dodge the issues you present to them, turning the conversation away from their conduct onto other subjects, telling you that your view about them is flawed and your perceptions about their aggression are misconceived.

Others of you may simply become disillusioned at the way in which your team meetings are consistently hijacked by the bully, wasting everyone's time and energy. You don't confront the bully because you feel intimidated, and you don't speak with your manager about the situation because you are aware of how poorly they are handling the issues and don't wish to draw attention to their lack of skill at recognising or handling the bullying.

This chapter explores the issues facing you when one of your team colleagues targets your manager. It examines the negative impact the bully has on a team meeting, and identifies what you can do to make a positive contribution during the meeting. The chapter explores practical steps you could take to minimise the negative impact of the bullying on the process of the meeting, so that you offer support to the target and skilfully confront the bully. It highlights how to handle the challenging dynamics so that you don't become a silent witness to the bullying and enable it through your passivity, or inadvertently undermine your manager's authority by intervening clumsily on their behalf.

Consider the following case study.

Case Study 6: Negative Impact

A family-owned textile business employs fifty people, of whom six are supervisors responsible for managing the various production teams. Many of the company's employees are drawn from local families, and all of the current supervisors have followed their parents into the business.

The supervisors meet with the MD twice a day, at 8 am and 1 pm. The purpose of these meetings is to plan the day's work, compare the day's outputs against targets, and receive sales briefings from the MD. The MD has run the business for four years, taking over from her father on his retirement. Hard working and conscientious, she is an excellent saleswoman who takes seriously her company's responsibility to the families who rely on the business for employment. The MD is no fool. She can be hard-headed and resilient, and she is quite able to say 'no' and 'not yet' to the supervisors. The supervisors respect her integrity and work ethic, but quietly question her judgement behind her back on occasions when she accepts large orders without checking the production lead times with them in advance.

One of the six supervisors is female. The female supervisor is responsible for a team of ten production workers. She has worked for the company for over twenty years, longer than any of the other supervisors, and sees herself as their unofficial spokesperson. Over a period of two months, she starts to groom the MD. The female supervisor seeks out the MD in her office for a series of short one-to-one meetings. The MD's office overlooks the production floor. At first, when the female supervisor begins visiting her office, the MD is open to the impromptu meetings. On each occasion, the female supervisor knocks on the door, enters the office straightaway and engages the MD in a direct and apparently relevant discussion about production schedules or specific orders. The MD forms the view that the female supervisor wants to alert her to developing issues on the production floor, and to issues which the rest of the supervisors may want to raise with her during their twice daily meetings. But, towards the end of the second month of the frequent visits from the female supervisor, events take an unwelcome and nasty turn.

During the mid-morning rush on a particularly busy Monday, the female supervisor enters the MD's office without knocking. Using a cold and cutting tone, she tells the MD that she needs to alert her to the fact that 'her latest big sell is putting the workforce under pressure and they are kicking back.' She pauses briefly, before telling the MD that the supervisors are questioning her judgement and that she ought to be prepared for a barrage of questions at the one o'clock briefing. The MD is taken aback by both the supervisor's tone and her uncompromising message. She composes herself quickly, tells the supervisor that she will handle the meeting, thanks her for alerting her to the issues, and returns to the paperwork on her desk. The supervisor pauses for a moment, notes that the MD is visibly shaken, smiles to herself and leaves the office.

The female supervisor is already in the meeting room when the MD arrives for the one o'clock meeting later that day. It is the MD's habit to arrive in the meeting room ten minutes before the start of each briefing, so that she can arrange her papers and get ready. The MD is slightly surprised that the female supervisor is already seated in the room when she arrives, but thinks nothing of it. The MD starts the meeting on time by acknowledging that she understands that the production deadlines on the latest order are tight, but that she is certain that the workforce will pull together to ensure that the order goes out on time. At this point, using a peremptory and humiliating tone, the female supervisor launches an attack on her employer in front of her colleagues. She refers to the MD's 'ill-considered and fundamentally defective management of the business' and describes the latest deadlines that her team need to meet as 'ludicrous.' The other five supervisors are shocked by this turn of events. While none of them is comfortable with the tight deadlines that their production teams are working to, none of them would go so far as to describe the MD's management of the business as fundamentally flawed. Each of the five other supervisors either shifts uncomfortably in their seats or remains still and silent, waiting to see what will happen next.

The MD picks up the glass of water in front of her and takes a sip. Placing the glass back on the table, she looks the female supervisor in the eye and tells her in an even-handed but firm tone that she understands that the production teams are working flat out. She tells her supervisor that the latest order is the first of at least three large orders from the same customer, and it is important that the first one is fulfilled on time and to standard. The MD fully expects her logical and straightforward argument to settle the matter and is taken by surprise when the female supervisor draws breath a second time. Using the same cutting, cold tone she tells the MD that she is not sufficiently on top of the mood of the production floor, and needs to spend some time with the workforce. The MD thanks her for her input, says she will do so over the coming week, and proceeds to the first item on the agenda.

Over the next two weeks, each of the two daily briefings follows the same pattern. The female supervisor attacks the MD and her management of the business, citing a number of reasons to back up her criticisms. None of the issues she hones in on is a real concern for the production teams or the company. Each of them is a pretext to bully. She tells the MD that she ought to consider upgrading the lighting on the production floor. She says that there is an urgent need to re-assess the chemical composition of the dyes used in carpet production. She claims that the rota should be altered so that each production team has two longer afternoon breaks per week rather than one. The female supervisor provides numerous 'reasons' to back up her view that each of these measures should be adopted, and while she is speaking, each of the other supervisors appears impatient or perplexed. None of them speaks either in support of her argument or against it, partly out of deference to the MD whom they like and whom they expect to act decisively to prevent the waste of their time, and partly because they are intimidated by the female supervisor's aggression. Towards the end of a lengthy explanation about the merits of changing the invoicing date from the third Monday to the second Tuesday in the month, the most recently appointed supervisor tells the female supervisor that while the changes she proposes would result in things being done differently, he doesn't think they will make any material difference to the quality of the work done by the production teams or the effectiveness of the company. The female supervisor turns towards him and, in withering tones, accuses him of always wanting to have his own way. The newly appointed supervisor is floored by this assessment of his character and does not know what to say next. He looks around the room for support, notes the averted eyes of each of his four other supervisor colleagues, and is defeated. He remains silent throughout the rest of the meeting.

The MD also remains largely silent throughout the bullying. When she does speak, her objective comments and logical questions are brushed aside by the female supervisor. The MD is shocked to hear her management of the company, and particularly her successful sales work, described as 'evidence of poor decision-making' and as 'taking us down the wrong path.' Worn down by the criticisms and haranguing of an employee with whom she thought she had a productive working relationship, the MD adopts the ineffective strategy of letting the female supervisor finish what she is saying before trying to take the meeting back to the business it is there to discuss.

On each occasion that the meeting runs over-time with the agenda only half-completed, the MD suggests that she and the female supervisor meet later in her office to complete discussion of her concerns. When the issues are parked in this way, the five supervisors who remain inadvertent passive enablers of the bullying take a collective sigh of relief. But when the MD and female supervisor meet to discuss the latter's concerns in the MD's office, the bullying continues. In a series of escalating attacks, the female supervisor tells her employer that she 'doesn't know how to handle the supervisors' and that 'she isn't half the MD her father was.'

One month into the campaign of bullying, and after a particularly fraught and time-consuming daily meeting, one of the supervisors remarks to another that the female supervisor seems to be 'coming on a bit strong.' Both supervisors are at their workstations, but neither of them is able to concentrate on their duties. Like all the non-bullying supervisors, they feel disturbed at the direction the daily briefings are taking, at the waste of time that occurs every time the female supervisor starts to attack the MD, and at the way the MD appears not to know how to prevent her bullying employee from pursuing her topic-of-the-day. Stuck between wanting to support the MD, and not knowing how to do so without incurring the wrath of the female supervisor, all five non-bullying supervisors remain silent during the meetings and often leave without the information or the direction they need. Without adequate briefings, they start to feel pressurised and make mistakes in their supervision of the production teams. During the fifth week of the female supervisor's campaign, four of the five teams do not meet their production targets for that week. The following week, three of the four teams fail to make up the lost output. The production teams feel under increasing pressure and start to grumble about their workloads. They complain to their supervisors about the strain they feel under. The non-bullying supervisors talk to one another about the issues, but don't feel able to speak directly to the MD for fear of opening up a can of worms. Over the next month, production targets are not met by five of the six teams. Although the big order which so excited the MD is fulfilled on time, the customer queries the standard of some of the work and does not place the expected two repeat orders.

Analysing the Dynamics in Case Study 6: Negative Impact

In this case study, a conscientious and hard-working MD is subject to workplace bullying from one of her supervisors during twice daily team briefings. Each attack is conducted in full view of the other five supervisors in the company. Neither the MD nor the non-bullying supervisors know how to respond effectively at the time. The MD is taken in by the 'reasons' presented by the bullying supervisor during her attacks, each of which is a pretext for her campaign of bullying. Unable to recognise the bullying for what it is, the MD listens to each of the increasingly lengthy arguments put forward by the bully, and tries to reason with her. Her logical responses are brushed aside by the bullying supervisor so, in an attempt to prevent further wasted time, the MD suggests that the two of them could continue their discussion after the team briefing. This well-intentioned but ineffective strategy only sets her up for further bullying in her office later that day.

During the attacks, the non-bullying supervisors are largely ineffective bystanders. They sit back and let events unfold around them. They take this tack partly because they expect their MD to manage the situation even though it is quickly apparent that she doesn't know how to, and partly because they abrogate responsibility for helping her to intervene effectively. When the newest supervisor does try to intervene, suggesting that the arguments put forward by the female supervisor are not likely to make a material difference to the company's work, she turns on him, characterising him as someone who always wants his own way. He looks around the table for support from the other supervisors, sees only averted eyes and gives up. The passivity of the non-bullying supervisors - a direct result of how intimidated they feel by the female supervisor's aggression - results in them failing to support either the MD when she is attacked or the newest supervisor when he attempts to confront the bully.

Over a period of two months, each team briefing is hijacked by the bully who uses it as a vehicle to castigate the MD in a series of escalating attacks on her leadership of the business. On each occasion, the supportive but passive supervisors don't intervene. As the bullying continues, the twice daily briefings fail to address the business issues they are there to discuss. The supervisors leave without the information or direction they need, and the MD becomes worn out by the constant haranguing and abuse she receives from the bullying supervisor. Eventually, production is affected. Several teams miss their production targets, and while the company's major order is fulfilled, the customer is not satisfied with the standard of the work, and does not place a repeat order. The campaign of bullying, which targets the MD, is allowed to take up so much management energy and supervisory time that it affects the company's ability to serve its customers.

As the previous chapter explored strategies which the MD could employ to confront the bullying, we will examine these only briefly. The rest of this chapter will then focus on what the non-bullying supervisors could do to make a positive contribution to the situation evolving around them in the daily briefings.

Mishandling a Campaign of Bullying

It is true to say that the MD misjudges the visits which the female supervisor makes to her office. She fails to recognise them for what they are, a series of grooming encounters. Unaware that she has been successfully groomed, the MD then makes a second mistake and fails to see the female supervisor's aggressive attacks during the twice daily briefings for what they are, a campaign of workplace bullying. She mishandles the moment during the attacks on her in her office, and allows each of the twice daily briefings to become a vehicle for bullying. Instead of managing each meeting effectively so that it provides her supervisors with the information and direction they need, the MD allows her energy to be dissipated as she fends off the bullying supervisor, and permits her supervisors' time to be wasted.

The female supervisor finds it easy to create a bullying dynamic in her relationship with her employer partly because the MD responds to the bullying ineffectively, and partly because the other supervisors at the meeting adopt the role of passive observers of the bullying. Between them, the MD and the non-bullying supervisors get it completely wrong. They allow the crucial daily briefings to be hijacked by the bully to such an extent that eventually there is an adverse impact on production.

Let's focus on effective steps which any of the non-bullying supervisors could employ to simultaneously:

- Prevent the bully from dominating the twice daily meetings.

- Support their MD at the time of the attacks.

- Reduce the possibility that they will be targeted next.

Refusing to Become a Passive Enabler

When the bullying supervisor commences her campaign, it is imperative that each supervisor decides to take an active part in the process of the meeting at the time of each attack. Each of them needs to speak up and confront the bullying in an effective manner for two reasons. Firstly, they need to demonstrate to the bully that she is outnumbered and outmatched, a set of circumstances which is likely to give her serious pause for thought. Secondly, they each need to send her a clear message that they will not be an easy person for her to target outside the meeting.

Failure to confront her bullying will work against each of the non-bullying supervisors in three ways. Firstly, their time will be wasted during the meeting, and their ability to perform to standard will be compromised as they will not gain the clear direction they need for that day's work. Secondly, they make it more likely – not less likely – that the bully will see them as a soft target and consider bullying them outside the meeting. Thirdly, their failure to confront the castigation of their MD's leadership could be taken as tacit approval of the bullying comments, and be used against them at a later date by the bully. It may seem risky for them to speak up, but it much more risky for them to remain passive enablers of workplace bullying.

The bullying supervisor will be encouraged as soon as she learns that she will not be confronted by her peer group when she attacks the MD. While none of the non-bullying supervisors *actually wants* to enable the bullying of the MD, that is exactly what they do when they remain silent and disengaged during the bullying. The bullying supervisor recognises that not only does the MD not know how to repel her attacks, but neither do any of the other supervisors. Her way is clear to continue her campaign, and escalate it whenever she wants to.

Each non-bullying supervisor needs to recognise that they have a responsibility to act decisively once the bullying starts, and once it becomes clear that their MD does not know how to respond effectively at the time. They may be reluctant to assume this responsibility, perhaps held back by a concern that intervening might inadvertently undermine the authority of their MD or annoy her. However, they need to keep in mind that their MD is having a hard time asserting her authority in the meeting, and is permitting it to be hijacked by the bully. It is time for the non-bullying supervisors to put aside their concerns about how their input may be received by the MD. It is their responsibility to take steps to protect the integrity of the daily team briefings, so that each of them can continue to leave the meeting with the information they need to set direction for their production teams. Having made the decision to become actively involved in the meeting at the time of the attacks, each supervisor needs to employ strategies which are effective in confronting the bully, and respectful towards the MD.

Don't become a passive enabler of bullying in your team. It's better to confront the bullying safely and effectively.

Active Involvement

Each supervisor needs to sit upright throughout the meeting, leaning slightly forward at the table. This stance will tell the bully that each of them is actively involved in the process of the meeting, and that none of them will abrogate their responsibility towards it. Employing a clear and firm tone, every time the bully launches an attack on the MD, one of the non-bullying supervisors needs to:

- Inform the bully that her aggression is out of step with the meeting and needs to cease.

- Tell her that the MD has a set agenda for the meeting which they have successfully followed for a long time.

- Point out to her that the purpose of the meeting is to plan the day's work, compare the day's outputs against targets, and receive sales briefings from the MD.

- Inform her that since her input is not about any of the agenda topics, but is about changes she wants to see made to the way the company operates, she needs to cease making her comments at the daily supervisors' meetings.

If the bullying supervisor ignores this feedback, or tests the resolve of the speaker by making another aggressive criticism of the MD or him, the non-bullying supervisor needs to reinforce his point immediately. He could do this by using an emphatic and decisive tone and telling her firstly, that he is going to repeat what he just said because it appears that he hasn't got his message across yet; and secondly, that he does not want his time wasted by her taking the meeting away from the business it is there to discuss.

This approach makes it clear that the speaker respects the authority of the MD and sees her as the person in charge of the meeting. It opens up the possibility that the MD will reinforce what he has just said and exert her authority in the meeting. Above all, it clarifies that the purpose of the meeting is to discuss business matters. It places on the table the fact that since the bullying supervisor does not want to discuss business matters, her input represents a clear waste of the time for everyone in the room. It puts the issue of her involvement in the meeting back to the bully, telling her that the tone and content of her bullying criticisms are unwelcome. It gives her a clear choice: keep attacking the MD and keep being confronted, or stop. This approach avoids the pitfalls of:

- Obviously defending the leadership of the MD, a tactic which would result in the bully attacking the supervisor who speaks up.

- Opposing the bully or her opinions which would simply result in her inventing additional 'reasons' to justify her point of view, and escalate the bullying.

- Undermining the authority of the MD by saying that she is being bullied at the meeting.

- Embarrassing the MD by failing to acknowledge that it is her meeting.

Instead, this carefully-crafted strategy gives the bully a clear choice. It requires that she:

- Recognise that her use of aggression is in the spotlight.

- Confine her remarks to the business of the meeting.

- Restrict her input to production matters only, and cease using the meeting to make personal criticisms of the MD and her leadership.

However, it is likely that the bullying supervisor will initially ignore this feedback and, at some point in the meeting, resume her attack on the MD. When this happens, the same message needs to be repeated a second, and then a third, and if necessary a fourth time. It would be preferable for each of the non-bullying supervisors to take a turn at articulating the same message. The non-bullying supervisors can afford to invest time during this phase of the confrontation. They need to continually repeat their key message i.e. that the participants in the meeting will not let the bullying supervisor hijack it with her personal agenda. The aim of repeating this message - over and over again if necessary - is to make it clear to the bullying supervisor that her colleagues are not going to let her bully. It is a matter of willpower, and they will need to be determined.

Of course, not all five non-bullying supervisors may be ready to stand up to the bully. Some of them may wait to see how events unfold before electing to join their peers in confronting the bully. But, assuming that at least one non-bullying supervisor finds the courage to speak up in the first instance, it is likely that others will take heart from his resolve and join him. It is not necessary for the non-bullying supervisors to agree in advance to take this course of action, although they could do so. Each of them simply needs to make up his own mind to act with resolve and clarity, and draw a clear boundary around the bully's involvement with the meeting.

Those supervisors who speak up need to:

- Use an uncompromising tone.

- Appear unafraid of the bullying supervisor.

- Recognise that by confronting the bully in this business-focused way they are offering life-giving support to the MD.

> **Inform the bully that their aggression is out of step with the meeting.**

> **Remind the bully of the agenda and purpose of the meeting. Inform them that they need to confine their input to the topics on the agenda.**

> **Keep repeating the message until the bully has heard it. The more non-bullying members who speak, the quicker it will be for the bully to realise they are outnumbered and outmatched.**

Let's examine each of these factors in turn.

Uncompromising Tone

In order to interrupt her flow, each supervisor who confronts the bully needs to use a tone which conveys that he is not at all pleased at having his time wasted, that he is not going to sit still while the bullying supervisor uses aggression to control the meeting, and that he is quite determined that the meeting will focus only on the production issues it is there to discuss. The tone of each supervisor who conveys this message is vital. He needs to use an uncompromising tone, one which denotes that he is not intimidated by the bully, is resolute in his desire that the meeting return to the set agenda, and that he is not going to take 'no' for an answer. It is his *will* that he needs to convey through his adamant tone, and his will is that the bullying supervisor stop talking and let the meeting proceed according to plan.

Appearing Resolute, Standing Together

The bullying supervisor is one person in a meeting of seven. She is the most aggressive and persistent speaker in the room, and the one who is most out of step with the purpose of the meeting. Her desire to speak at length on topics which have nothing to do with the business of the meeting represents a clear opportunity for any of the other supervisors to challenge her control. It is vital that the bully get the clear message that her aggression towards the MD does not unsettle the supervisors and does not intimidate them, even though it clearly does unsettle the MD who is unable to respond effectively to her tactics. In truth, some or all, of the supervisors may be intimidated, but they must find a way to put their fear to one side during the confrontation and *appear* resolute.

Every time the bully is tempted to test their resolve and reintroduce her bullying agenda by making an aggressive or demeaning remark to the MD, one of the supervisors needs to be prepared to jump straight in and confront her. He must not worry that he may undermine the MD by doing this. Her position as the person chairing the meeting is already compromised by her inability to handle the bullying, and his intervention is designed to assist her. Each supervisor needs to recognise that by intervening skilfully, he makes a positive contribution to the situation, supports the MD without undermining her, and changes the momentum of the meeting. At the moment, each of the non-bullying supervisors and the MD stands alone. When the MD is bullied, no one intervenes. When the newest supervisor tries to intervene, no one supports him. This pernicious cycle results in the bully having it all her own way, while each of the participants at the meeting permits bullying in their midst. The starting point for changing this pattern of behaviour is for one person to stand up to the bully effectively. Since the MD is not able to do so, this task falls to one of the supervisors in the room. The supervisor who decides to speak needs to remind the bullying supervisor – in ever more emphatic tones – that her input is only welcome if it addresses production issues. Let's examine why this is so pivotal.

The bullying supervisor thrives on the non-confrontational style of the MD. She takes heart from her employer's preference for logical debate, and finds it easy to brush aside the MD's reasoned arguments. Equally, she finds it straightforward to crush the newest supervisor when he tries to question her judgement. She attacks him straight back. But being confronted by up to five colleagues who are unafraid of her – or who appear to be unafraid of her – and who doggedly want the meeting to focus on production issues only, will present her with quite a different challenge. She will either have to take on up to five colleagues at the same time, which will be difficult for her to do, or she will need to restrict her remarks to production matters only. It is highly likely that she will do the prudent thing and cease bullying the MD during the meeting. This will enable the meeting to progress according to the agenda, and go a long way to preventing the company from sending sub-standard work to it's major customer.

Offering Life-Giving Support

Being supported in the moment of an attack will give vital encouragement to the MD. She will know that the sentiment of at least some of the supervisors in the meeting is to back her up. She will gain much strength from this knowledge, will learn that challenging the bully's willpower is a more effective tactic than debating the 'reasons' with her, and is likely to gain fresh impetus to confront the bullying outside of the daily briefing meeting. The benefit to the supervisors of handling things this way is that none of them needs to broach the subject of her being bullied with the MD, a conversation which would inevitably put the MD on the back foot, will be an awkward discussion to have, and may well undermine the MD's authority further as she hears her supervisors question her handling of the female supervisor. Now that she knows that some or all of the non-bullying supervisors are actively standing against the bullying, this will give her options for re-asserting her authority with the bully.

Summary of Key Points from the Chapter

It can be highly challenging to have a bully in your team, one who targets your manager or supervisor during team meetings. This is especially true if your manager doesn't know how to respond effectively to the attacks at the time they occur. In this case, your

---

manager's credibility will be compromised, the time of all of the non-bullying team members wasted, and the team meeting could fail to achieve its objectives. In some circumstances, depending on the purpose of the meeting, this situation could evolve into a crisis as production is negatively affected and customers become dissatisfied.

You may want your team manager to handle the bullying effectively, and relieve you of the need to sit through a meeting which wastes your time. You may also regard it as your manager's responsibility to handle the bully effectively so you don't have to. But, it is also *your* responsibility, as a member of the meeting at which bullying is occurring, to act decisively each and every time the bully uses aggression or tries to dominate the meeting. It is your responsibility to take a stand and confront the bully, especially if your manager doesn't know how to. Taking the role of passive enabler will not work well for you, or for your team. It increases the likelihood of you becoming a target for the bully in the future, makes it easier for the bully to bully in the team meeting, and sets up the possibility that the bully may use your silence against you at a later date. Remaining silent and passive when bullying occurs at your team meeting is risky. It is better to confront the bullying using a carefully-crafted approach, one which enables you to stand against the bully without undermining your manager.

The more people in your team meeting who are willing to confront the bully, the easier it will be for the team to contain and manage the bullying. Between you, you need to send the bully the consistent and clear message that they need to stick to the agenda of the meeting. Every time the bully attacks your manager, you need to inform them that their aggression is out of step with the meeting and needs to cease, reiterate the real purpose of the meeting, and tell them to confine their comments to those topics only. This approach not only presents the bully with a clear choice – keep bullying and keep being confronted, or stop bullying – it also avoids a series of pitfalls which would exacerbate the situation.

The tools available to you as you confront the bully are your active involvement in the process of the meeting, your use of an uncompromising tone, and your ability to appear resolute and unafraid. The greater the number of your peers who are prepared to join you in confronting the bully, the easier it will be for the bully to come to the conclusion that they are outnumbered and outmatched. Your aim in confronting the bullying is three-fold: to prevent the bully from hijacking the meeting, to support your manager without having to discuss the issues with them directly, and to reduce the likelihood that you may be targeted at a future date inside or outside the meeting.

Handling the issues in this way will result in your manager receiving much-needed support. You don't need to agree with your peers in advance that you will, between you, handle things in this way, but you can do so if you know some or all of them well enough. The fact that one of you stands up to the bully will encourage those of your peer group who are initially reluctant to speak out, and add to the pressure on the bully to stop wasting everyone's time and let the meeting proceed to plan.

Questions for You to Consider

You may now like to apply the material from this chapter to your own working life. Bring to mind a specific situation in which you observed a member of your team bullying your manager (or supervisor) at a team meeting. You can jot down your answers to each of the following questions in the space below it:

1. Who bullied your manager (or supervisor)? At which team meeting did the bully attack?

2. How did your manager (or supervisor) respond to the bullying at the time it occurred?

3. What impact did the bullying have on the process of the team meeting?

4. How did you, as a participant in the meeting, respond at the time the bullying occurred?

5. To what extent did your response influence the situation positively?

6. Looking back on it now, what could you have said or done differently that would have made a more positive contribution to the situation?

Next Chapter

Chapter 9 focuses on the issues involved in weighing up the pros and cons of remaining in a situation of on-going abuse, or deciding to leave your job.

Chapter 9
Making a Positive Choice

Leaving Your Job or Remaining in Your Role

A Situation of On-going Abuse

You recognise that there is much you can do to confront the bullying you are subject to. You have tools in your toolkit for addressing the bullying, for using self-preserving and self-protective behaviour at the time of an attack, and you know how to alter the bullying dynamic in your favour. There are more skills you can develop and practise in the coming days and weeks. But the question uppermost in your mind is: do you want to? You are asking yourself: do you want to spend a proportion of your energy at work, possibly on a daily basis, repelling attacks orchestrated against you by a workplace bully? Do you want to experience your workplace as taxing for the wrong reasons? While you are up for handling constructive challenge as part of your role - perhaps through the need to handle demanding, non-bullying customers or learn complex skills – do you want to handle bullying behaviour on a consistent or occasional basis as a part of that job? Maybe you want to experience your workplace as comfortable enough that the greater part of your energy goes towards handling your duties effectively. And, if that is currently not the case, and you are utilising precious energy dealing with abusive encounters no matter how effectively you are handling them, you may be starting to ask yourself whether your future doesn't lie elsewhere.

However, that train of thought opens up a series of uncomfortable issues for you. While you may be starting to wonder whether you wouldn't be better off working somewhere else, you are wary of the prospect of leaving your current employer. Part of you thinks that it is the bully who should give up their job, not you. You may feel resentful that the bully continues blithely in their role, while it is you who is actively considering giving up yours. This injustice may rankle with you, and it adds to the complexity of your decision about whether to stay or go. If you do leave, you want to do so as a progressive choice but you don't quite know how to turn what feels like a potential negative into a positive.

This chapter will help you step back from your situation and evaluate the options as you make your decision about whether to stay or go. It examines how to weigh up the four critical components of what you *feel* about your workplace, what you *need* from it, what *resources* are available to you, and what *choices* you have so you can act in your highest, best interests. The chapter outlines a mind-set to adopt so that, whether you decide to remain in your current role or leave your employer to work elsewhere, you do so from a position of strength, as positive choice.

The Issues Involved in Leaving Your Job

Even though you have learned how to repel bullying attacks at the time they occur, and therefore protect yourself from some or all of the impact of the bullying, you may still think it is time to consider leaving your current job. Those of you who work for a large employer may be able to search for a different job in the same organisation. Those of you who work for a smaller employer, or who perform a more specialist role, may need to leave your organisation altogether and seek employment elsewhere. However, neither of these options may be a straightforward course of action to take, especially if your well-being has been negatively impacted as a result of bullying.

You may feel considerable resentment about the option of leaving. You may take the view that it is deeply unfair that you need to give up your employment to protect yourself from a workplace bully. You may have lost some self-esteem or self-confidence, and the prospect of 'losing your job' may be psychologically challenging for you. Alternatively, you may be concerned that, as a result of being bullied, your energy levels have dipped. You don't know if you can easily find the inner resources to look for another job. You may also have to face the fact that your self-confidence is lower than usual, and you might not present well at a selection interview. Some of you may actually feel quite down at the prospect of looking for alternative employment. You may worry that any future workplace could be just as unsafe as your present one, and that you'd be better off staying in your current job where at least you know what you are dealing with.

But the fact remains that your best interests may be better served elsewhere, and looking for alternative employment is an option you need to consider.

Others of you may want to leave your current employer, but don't know how to make the experience of departing a positive one. You don't want to feel as if you are running away from a difficult situation, a frame of mind which would leave you feeling defeated, weak or ashamed. You want to leave for positive reasons, to create a better experience of the workplace, and because you want to take control of your life. You are considering what reasons to give to your current employer to explain your wish to leave. Do you say you are leaving because of bullying at work? Or do you simply leave without putting these issues on the table?

The Issues Involved in Remaining in Your Job

There may be many reasons why you want to remain in your job. You may have worked for your employer for a long time and feel loyal to them. You may have financial imperatives which result in you needing your present income or you may consider that, even though you are being bullied, leaving would involve too great a loss. You may not want to lose colleagues whom you value and like. You may not want to lose clients or suppliers with whom you have worked for a long time and who respect you. You may not want to incur the upheaval and the unknown of a new role at a time when your inner resources are stretched dealing with workplace bullying. Taking on a new role elsewhere brings with it the possibility of failure, or of performing less effectively than at present. You'd have to re-establish credibility with new colleagues, a new manager and new clients. These factors may represent a step too far. You conclude that looking for a different role with another employer is not a viable option for you.

The Role of Feelings, Needs, Resources and Choices in Making a Positive Decision

Alternatively, you may consider the prospect of working elsewhere to be quite energising. You may look favourably on the options of a new challenge, a fresh start and new colleagues. Your spirits may lift, and you may take much heart, from the option of leaving behind the bullying culture you currently work in and starting again somewhere else.

Whichever way your thoughts are tending – to remain in your current role or move to alternative employment - you want to make a positive decision. You need a process to help you sift through the options and find a productive way forward. Consider the following diagram.

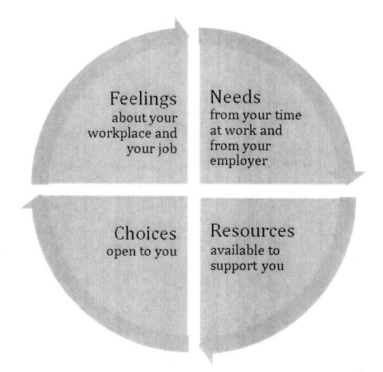

Diagram 3: The relationship between your feelings, needs, resources and choices

The framework encourages you to make distinctions between what:

- You *feel* about your workplace and your role at work.

- You *need* from your time in the workplace and from your employer.

- *Resources* are available to you to help you cope with the bullying.

- *Choices* are open to you as you decide how to handle your situation.

You can see that there are arrows around the outside of each of the four segments, denoting the inter-connections between what you feel, what you need, the resources at your disposal, and the choices open to you.

You will have an opportunity to complete the framework for yourself shortly. When doing so, it is important to clarify your feelings first. Write down everything you feel about the workplace and your role. Take your time about this. As you start to write down the feelings which are uppermost in your mind, you will get in touch with deeper feelings, perhaps including feelings you didn't know you had. Give yourself time to identify all of your feelings fully before you move on to the second section.

Next, write down what you need. Some of your needs may flow directly from what you feel. For instance, if you feel afraid or anxious at work, then what you need is to feel safe or comfortable. Include needs you have of your employer which are not about the bullying. These may include a need to learn new skills or to work with people you like and connect well with.

Then, write down the resources available to you inside and outside of work. Include those resources which you are able to access – like the support of friends and family - as well as those which you may not have used yet, such as the option of making a formal complaint.

Next, write down all the choices available to you. Include options you may not want to put into practice, like re-training for a new job or taking a period of sick leave.

Finally, decide which of the choices – or which combination of choices – best meets your needs and represents the optimum way forward for you. Highlight this choice on the diagram.

> **Clarify your feelings about your job, what you need from work, what resources are available to you, and what choices are open to you.**

In a moment I will ask you to complete your own framework but first let's explore how it works using three short examples.

Unresolved Situations

- An engineer is subject to workplace bullying from one of the managers in the firm he works for. He observes one colleague resign as a result of the bullying she is subject to by the same manager. The engineer decides to report the bullying manager to the firm's executives and submits a formal complaint to HR. He hopes that once the senior people in the firm are aware of the bullying they will take action against the manager. At the same time, he vigorously challenges the bullying every time it occurs. One month after submitting the formal complaint, the engineer contacts HR to enquire what steps have been taken as a result. He is told that 'the matter is in hand'. Six weeks later, with the bullying on-going and no further information available from HR about how his complaint will be handled, the engineer realises that the complaint may not be investigated at all. The engineer is a loyal man, and he feels dismayed. He has worked for the firm all his adult life. He comes to the conclusion that he does not want to work for a firm which condones bullying by failing to investigate a complaint. Even though he feels he is abandoning his colleagues to the bully, and does not have an alternative job to go to, he resigns hoping that his track record and qualifications will result in him finding alternative employment quickly.

- A female PA in a management consultancy firm is bullied by one of her male peers. The bully sits at the workstation next to hers. He makes nasty comments to the female PA's face, and slanders her behind her back. The female PA's reputation is affected as colleagues choose to believe the slander without checking out the facts with her. She becomes aware that colleagues who used to speak openly to her are guarded around her, and that people who used to invite her to lunch cease doing so. She feels excluded from social situations at work, and her self-esteem drops. She visits her GP, and takes time away from the workplace with work-related stress. While off work, she considers her position, including the possibility of resigning. Her time away from the workplace enables her to gain a new perspective on her situation, and she decides that she does not want to leave her job. Instead, she returns to work, determined to clear her name, confront the bullying, and regain the good opinion of her colleagues around the office.

- A fireman is subject to bullying from his watch commander. He initially considers leaving his role, but after talking it over with his partner and friends, decides to stay. The nearest fire station is fully staffed, he does not want to re-locate his family to another part of the county, and he does not want to ask his children to switch schools. He decides to stay for positive reasons: to enable his family to live in a house they like, going to schools they are settled in, and to continue to do a job he enjoys. The fireman makes a point of putting the issues back to the bully each and every time he is attacked and, over a period of three months, the frequency of the bullying abates. However, the fireman remains vigilant whenever he is at work.

In the first example, the engineer makes a formal complaint for workplace bullying against a manager in a firm he has worked for all his adult life. He fully expects the complaint to be investigated, especially since one colleague has already resigned as a result of being attacked by the same bullying manager. The engineer is dismayed that the firm does not investigate his complaint. He feels responsible for the welfare of colleagues who are also subject to bullying behaviour from the same manager, and does not want to abandon them. But when he realises that the executives in the firm are condoning bullying by their inaction, he decides to leave on principle. He does not have alternative employment to go to but, more importantly, he does not want to work for a firm which enables bullying. His framework is shown in diagram 4 overleaf:

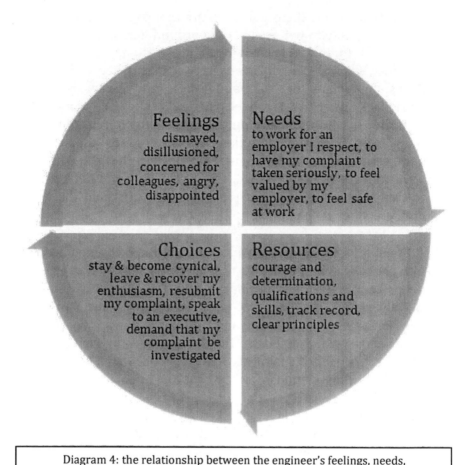

Feelings
dismayed,
disillusioned,
concerned for
colleagues, angry,
disappointed

Needs
to work for an
employer I respect, to
have my complaint
taken seriously, to feel
valued by my
employer, to feel safe
at work

Choices
stay & become cynical,
leave & recover my
enthusiasm, resubmit
my complaint, speak
to an executive,
demand that my
complaint be
investigated

Resources
courage and
determination,
qualifications and
skills, track record,
clear principles

Diagram 4: the relationship between the engineer's feelings, needs,
resources and choices

In the second example, a female PA is bullied by a male peer. The bullying PA slanders the female PA so effectively that colleagues who used to like her now shun her, and she quickly finds herself left out of social situations at work. Her self-esteem plummets. During a period of time away from the workplace with a stress-related condition, the female PA gains a new perspective on her situation. She does consider leaving her job and starting again somewhere else, but decides against it. She decides to return to the workplace and regain her reputation. Although it will take energy and skill, she wants to remain in her job and alter the dynamics around her rather than leave with her reputation in tatters. Her framework is shown in diagram 5:

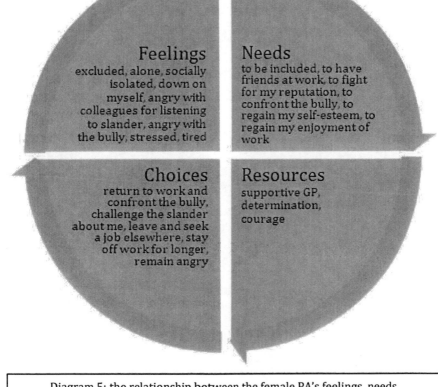

Feelings
excluded, alone, socially isolated, down on myself, angry with colleagues for listening to slander, angry with the bully, stressed, tired

Needs
to be included, to have friends at work, to fight for my reputation, to confront the bully, to regain my self-esteem, to regain my enjoyment of work

Choices
return to work and confront the bully, challenge the slander about me, leave and seek a job elsewhere, stay off work for longer, remain angry

Resources
supportive GP, determination, courage

Diagram 5: the relationship between the female PA's feelings, needs, resources and choices

In the third example, the fireman considers applying for a position at another fire station. But he is put off the idea by the fact that the nearest station is fully staffed, and a move elsewhere would require his children to switch schools, and his family to leave the house they like. He decides to stay in his current role for positive reasons, so that he can maintain his family in a lifestyle they enjoy. He repels each and every bullying attack that is made on him, and succeeds in reducing the frequency of the attacks. The bullying does abate, though the fireman needs to keep his wits about him when he is at work. He draws comfort from the fact that he is serving his family by taking this course of action, and from the fact that his ability to put the issues back to the bully is effective in reducing the level and intensity of the bullying. His framework is shown in diagram 6:

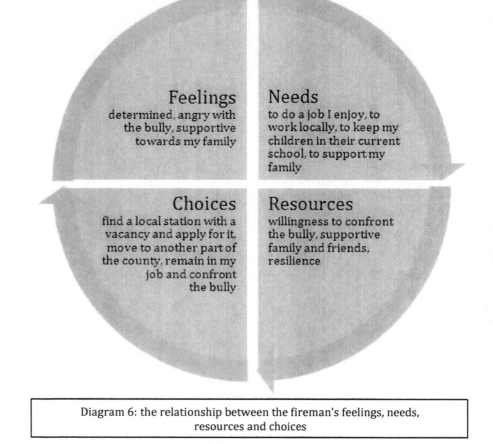

Feelings
determined, angry with
the bully, supportive
towards my family

Needs
to do a job I enjoy, to
work locally, to keep my
children in their current
school, to support my
family

Choices
find a local station with a
vacancy and apply for it,
move to another part of
the county, remain in my
job and confront
the bully

Resources
willingness to confront
the bully, supportive
family and friends,
resilience

Diagram 6: the relationship between the fireman's feelings, needs,
resources and choices

Your Feelings, Needs, Resources and Choices

You may now like to step back from your situation and complete the
framework in relation to yourself. Your aim is to identify how you
feel about your workplace and your role at work, what you need
from your time in the workplace and from your employer, what
resources are available to you at the moment, and the range of
choices you could make as you decide how to handle your situation.

The blank framework for you to complete is shown on page 235. As
you complete it, you may want to refer to the following lists of
possible feelings, needs, resources and choices to help get you
started. The lists are designed to be a starting point and are not

exhaustive. If you use them as a prompt, you could read through each list and underline the words and phrases which resonate with you, before writing them on the diagram which follows the last of the four lists. Alternatively, if you don't want to use the lists, you can proceed straight to the diagram itself.

Possible feelings:

Impatient	Puzzled	Irritated	Angry	Furious
Dismayed	Unhappy	Anxious	Ashamed	Determined
Confused	Disoriented	Bewildered	Frustrated	Downhearted
Courageous	Tired	Afraid	Excluded	Alone
Disheartened	Dissatisfied	Worried	Isolated	Tense
Stressed	Exhausted	Emboldened	Influential	Apprehensive
Reticent	Optimistic	Bold	Reluctant	Drained

Write the feelings you have selected into the first segment of the diagram on the page 235. Then return to select words from the next list which is on your possible needs from your time at work.

Possible needs:

To be effective	To be valued	To be trusted
To contribute	To be influential	To set direction
To generate momentum	To do quality work	To build rapport
To enjoy my colleagues	To feel safe	To be included
To have friends	To be respected	To be heard

| To learn new skills | To travel | To have a career path |
| To develop experience | To manage projects | To have friends at work |

Write the needs you have selected into the second segment of the diagram on the following page. Then return to select words from the next list which is on possible resources, which include your inner resources as well as sources of support from other people.

Supportive family members	A supportive colleague or HR advisor
Supportive friends	Access to an effective coach
A supportive manager	Courage, determination
Qualifications, skills	Experience in your job
Positive references	Effective CV
Contacts for finding another job	Desire to make a positive change
Your self-respect	Desire to make changes to your life

Write the resources you have selected into the third segment of the diagram on the following page. Then return to select words from the next list which is on possible choices open to you.

Possible choices:

Speak informally to HR	Make a formal complaint
Transfer to another role in my employer	Keep confronting the bully
Challenge colleagues who shun me	Resign without saying why
Resign and explain why	Talk to supportive colleagues

Regain my good opinion in the office	Re-submit a formal complaint
Take time away from the workplace	Take a period of sick leave
Retire and enjoy time away from work	Work with an effective coach
Re-train for a new role that excites me	Seek alternative employment

Write down all the choices which are open to you in the fourth segment of the diagram. It doesn't matter at this stage if the choices you select conflict with one another. For instance, you may have selected both 'speak informally to HR' and 'make take time away from the workplace'. At this stage, it's important not to cut down your options, but to keep all the possibilities on the table.

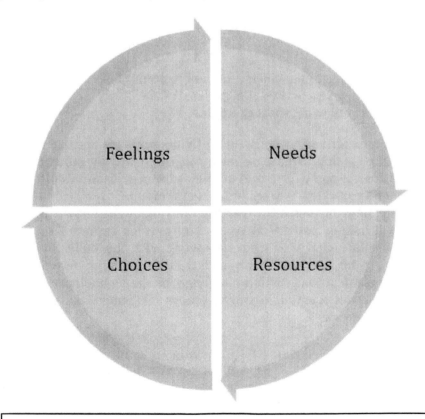

| Feelings | Needs |
| Choices | Resources |

Diagram 7: the relationship between your feelings, needs, resources and choices

We will return to the framework shortly so that you can re-visit the choices open to you and make a decision about the way forward. But first, let's explore the issues involved in developing a positive mind set.

Developing a Positive Mind-set

Whether you decide to stay in your current role, transition into another role with the same employer, or leave for a fresh start elsewhere, it is important that you do so with a positive mind-set. Key to the development of a positive mind-set is your perception that the choice you make enables you to:

- *Retain* something you want.

- *Gain* something which you don't currently have, but would value.

- *Achieve* something which you want to accomplish.

Consider the following short examples:

- After experiencing constant bullying from his manager for a period of four weeks, a technologist in an investment bank decides to apply for a role in one of the organisation's offices in another country. It takes him several months to secure the new role. He is sustained through the bullying by the knowledge that he is taking positive steps to improve his experience of the workplace, and won't have to work with the bully for much longer. His new role involves re-designing a large network and represents a considerable challenge for the technologist. But he has always wanted to travel, enjoys challenge, and wants to learn new skills.

- A stewardess is subject to bullying from the supervisor who handles her rota. The bully prevents her from taking her preferred annual leave dates, ensures she is placed on unfavourable night-flights which conflict with her family commitments, and is rude and disrespectful to her whenever they encounter one another. The stewardess enjoys her job, but is not prepared to compromise the quality of her family life for her job. She decides to re-evaluate her career choices. She leaves her employer, re-locates her young family to a rural part of the country she has always wanted to live in, and sets up a health food business with her partner. During her exit interview, she provides details about the bullying and unpleasant demeanour of the supervisor.

- A marketing manager in a supermarket chain is subject to bullying behaviour from a peer. In fact, the peer routinely bullies everyone in her own team, and anyone outside of it whom she can successfully groom. The marketing manager is determined not to let the bullying get to her. As the bullying peer does not have any direct input to the process of her work, the marketing manager thinks that, despite being subject to on-going bullying, she can continue to produce effective work and retain control over many aspects of her work experience. She decides that the best way to handle the bullying is to let the bully finish speaking, pass her hand over her head to denote that she is letting the words wash over her, and return to her work. She realises that the peer's habitual method of handling everyone at work is to bully them. This effective non-verbal riposte to the bullying enables her to maintain the standard of her work and she continues to deliver on time. She enjoys her job, does not want to make a life change, and remains committed to her employer and her job. She does not consider resigning.

In the first example, the technologist decides to transition roles within his employing organisation. In making this choice, he gains:

- New, non-bullying colleagues to work with.

- A fresh work challenge which will stretch and absorb him.

- The opportunity to learn new skills.

- The stimulation and excitement of living and working in another country.

In the second example, the stewardess decides to leave her employer and re-locate her family to a rural part of the country. In making these choices, she achieves:

- An improvement in her family's lifestyle.

- The rewards of spending more time with her children and partner.

- The autonomy and independence associated with running a business of her own.

- A greater degree of control over whom she works alongside.

In both cases, the choices the technologist and the stewardess make require considerable effort to implement. But they decide that making such positive changes to their lives is worth the effort and energy required. They both want to use their energy to invest in their futures, and both consider that using their inner resources to make life changes is a better use of that energy than expending it in dealing with bullying behaviour.

In the third example, the marketing manager does not consider leaving her role. In making this positive choice, she retains:

- A job which suits her and which she likes.

- Control over her experience of the workplace, making it quite clear to the bully that his tactics do not unsettle her or frighten her.

- The current balance of her life, obviating the major life upheaval associated with a change of role.

In this case, the mind-set which the marketing manager adopts consists of the view that she - and she alone - determines the quality of her experience at work. The bully may bully, and he does continue to do so, but she decides what attitude she will adopt. This way of looking at it enables her to keep doing the job she likes, and take satisfaction from the fact that the overall balance of her life is unaffected by the bullying.

Developing a positive mind-set is about clarifying what you retain, what you gain and what you achieve by taking the course of action you favour.

Your Positive Mind-set: Questions for You to Consider

You may now like to re-visit the diagram which you completed earlier in the chapter, so that you can reconsider the range of choices open to you and select a way forward. Take a moment to look back at the diagram before answering the following questions about it. Each question addresses one of the key issues for you to consider as you decide whether to stay in your current role or move to another job. You can jot down your answers in the space below each one.

1. Referring to your diagram: to what extent do the resources available to you support or sustain you while you handle the bullying?

2. Referring to your diagram: to what extent are your needs being met in your current job?

3. Referring to your diagram: how do your feelings about your work and your employer affect your life outside work?

4. Referring to your diagram: what choice or combination of choices represents the best way forward for you?

5. Referring to this choice or combination of choices: what will you gain by adopting this way forward?

6. Referring to this choice or combination of choices: what achievements does this way forward enable you to accomplish?

7. Referring to this choice or combination of choices: what positive factors will you retain by taking this approach?

Now that you have made your choice, give yourself some much earned credit. The issues you face as someone who is being bullied are challenging. They are demanding. One of the greatest sources of strength available to you is clarity about what you want to do. Making the decision you have made is an important step in bringing clarity to your situation. Act on your intention straightaway. Don't procrastinate. Take the first step, whether it's a mental adjustment in the way you think about your situation at work, or a practical action. You CAN do this. Don't delay. Take control.

Final Thoughts

The strategies and tools described in this book can and do work. Over the past twenty years, I have had the privilege of working with countless clients whose self-esteem plummeted as a result of being bullied. Each of them bounced back from a seemingly impossible situation.

If you are struggling to believe that you, too, can recover your confidence and enjoyment of the workplace, consider the following examples:

- A partner in a limited company was subject to workplace bullying by one of his peers. He was horrified that his workplace could become so unsafe, and furious that none of his senior colleagues stood with him to confront the bully. His confidence plummeted and his performance lowered. He was appalled that his partner colleagues harangued him for under-performing despite the fact that they all knew he was being bullied. He repeatedly confronted the bullying over a period of three months until he got the measure of his assailant and secured the upperhand in their encounters. Then he resigned. This was not a straightforward thing for him to do, as he had invested in the business. He sold his home and re-located his wife and family to another part of the country. He and his wife opened a small hotel. Their vision for their business included treating their employees, their customers, and one another with dignity and respect.

- An IT specialist was subject to workplace bullying at the insurance firm where he worked. He was crushed by the campaign, which was conducted openly and with the full knowledge of the senior managers in the firm. The IT specialist took time off work, learned assertiveness and confrontation skills, and returned to work ready to challenge his assailant. The bully was immediately unsettled by his new and more robust demeanour. Over a period of a few days, the IT specialist took charge of the interactions between them. Towards the end of their third meeting, the IT specialist leaned slightly forward across the desk and, using a clear and confident tone, said: 'I think we both know where we stand.' He took satisfaction from observing the bully's face go white, as he swallowed hard. The bullying did not resume.

- A secondary school teacher was bullied by her head of department, a much older and more experienced teacher. The secondary school teacher was completely floored that someone she had thought so highly of could turn on her in such a ruthless way. During coaching she worked on the intra-personal and inter-personal issues in her life that rendered her vulnerable to bullying. Over the next six months, she had trouble maintaining her performance levels, struggled to handle the more demanding children in her class, and worried that she would never be the same again. But, eventually, her hard work and effort were rewarded. She developed a more robust mind-set, and began to use different and more effective behaviour in her encounters with the bully. Over a period of a few weeks, the bullying reduced in intensity and then stopped altogether. The secondary school teacher remained on her guard, but no longer felt oppressed at work. She regained much of her enjoyment of teaching. The head of department learned to speak with her only when he had to, kept his interactions with her short and business focused, and otherwise left her to get on with her job.

-----------0-----------

To all of you who have read this far, I trust that reading this book has been rewarding for you. I hope that it has enabled you to acquire a different perspective on your experience of being bullied, a wider range of strategies for putting the issues back to the bully, and a greater number of options for preserving your personal power and using self-protective behaviour. I send you my best wishes for your journey to full recovery.

FREE Bonus Material on Workplace Bullying

- FREE access to a life-changing audio recording on recovery from workplace bullying

- FREE access to insightful, practical articles on responding effectively to bullying behaviour

- FREE access to manifestos on how to respond effectively to adversarial or bullying colleagues

- ...and much more

Register for instant FREE access now at:

www.oadeassociates.com/downloads